How to use exp

Issue 111

The 92 daily readings in this issue of *Explore* are designed to help you understand and apply the Bible as you read it each day.

It's serious!

We suggest that you allow 15 minutes each day to work through the Bible passage with the notes. It should be a meal, not a snack! Readings from other parts of the Bible can throw valuable light on the study passage. These cross-references can be skipped if you are already feeling full up, but will expand your grasp of the Bible. *Explore* uses the NIV2011 Bible translation, but you can also use it with the NIV1984 or ESV translations.

Sometimes a prayer box will encourage you to stop and pray through the lessons—but it is always important to allow time to pray for God's Spirit to bring his word to life, and to shape the way we think and live through it.

We're serious!

All of us who work on *Explore* share a passion for getting the Bible into people's lives. We fiercely hold to the Bible as God's word—to honour and follow, not to explain away.

1 Find a time you can read the Bible each day

2 Find a place where you can be quiet and think

3 Ask God to help you understand

4 Carefully read through the Bible passage for today

5 Study the verses with *Explore*, taking time to think

6 Pray about what you have read

thegoodbook
COMPANY

BIBLICAL | RELEVANT | ACCESSIBLE

Welcome to *explore*

Being a Christian isn't a skill you learn, nor is it a lifestyle choice. It's about having a real relationship with the living God through his Son, Jesus Christ. The Bible tells us that this relationship is like a marriage.

It's important to start with this, because it is easy to view the practice of daily Bible reading as a Christian duty, or a hard discipline that is just one more thing to get done in our busy lives.

But the Bible is God speaking to us: opening his mind to us on how he thinks, what he wants for us and what his plans are for the world. And most importantly, it tells us what he has done for us in sending his Son, Jesus Christ, into the world. It's the way that the Spirit shows Jesus to us, and changes us as we behold his glory.

Here are a few suggestions for making your time with God more of a joy than a burden:

- *Time:* Find a time when you will not be disturbed. Many people have found that the morning is the best time as it sets you up for the day. But whatever works for you is right for you.
- *Place:* Jesus says that we are not to make a great show of our religion *(see Matthew 6:5-6)*, but rather, to pray with the door to our room shut. Some people plan to get to work a few minutes earlier and get their Bible out in an office or some other quiet corner.
- *Prayer:* Although *Explore* helps with specific prayer ideas from the passage, do try to develop your own lists to pray through. Use the flap inside the back cover to help with this. And allow what you read in the Scriptures to shape what you pray for yourself, the world and others.
- *Feast:* You can use the "Bible in a year" line at the bottom of each page to help guide you through the entire Scriptures throughout 2025. This year, each day explores a different genre of the Bible. On Sundays, you'll read from a New Testament epistle; on Mondays, from the first five books of the Bible ("the Law"); Tuesdays cover Old Testament history books; Wednesdays enjoy the Psalms and Thursdays Old Testament poetry; Fridays focus on the prophets, and then on Saturdays you'll read through the Gospels. You can find the original version at bible-reading.com/bible-plan/html.
- *Share:* As the saying goes, *expression deepens impression.* So try to cultivate the habit of sharing with others what you have learned. Why not join our Facebook group to share your encouragements, questions and prayer requests? Search for *Explore: For your daily walk with God.*

And enjoy it! As you read God's word and God's Spirit works in your mind and your heart, you are going to see Jesus, and appreciate more of his love for you and his promises to you. That's amazing!

Carl Laferton is the Editorial Director of The Good Book Company

JAMES: The scattered life

Have you ever been far from home, felt a long way from safety and comfort, wished you had more friends around?

In many ways, that's a description of normal Christian experience—both today and in the mid-40s AD when James, the biological half-brother of Jesus himself, wrote the letter we're looking at for the next few weeks.

Claim to fame

Read James 1:1

- How does James describe himself?
- Given that James is the Lord Jesus' brother, why is this a little strange?
- What does it teach us about the importance and privilege of being Christ's servant?
- How does James describe the people of God, the "twelve tribes"?

Scattered: for discipline

Read Lamentations 4:11-16

This section of Jeremiah's lamentation over the destruction of Jerusalem by the army of King Nebuchadnezzar of Babylon describes the heart-breaking awfulness of the Lord's judgment on his people. They had been exiled from his land so they could see the seriousness of their sin.

- How is this judgment summed up (v 16)?
- How would it have felt to be scattered in this way?

TIME OUT

When we feel far from God and our fellow believers, it's worth asking: is the Lord disciplining me, to bring me back to humble obedience to him? We often blame God when he seems far away, and forget to ask if it's us who have wandered from a daily walk with him!

Scattered: for blessing

Read Acts 8:4; 11:19

- What does this scattering achieve?

The first Christians were scattered among the nations. They suffered greatly—but were also the way that God reached the lost. One day the Lord Jesus will return to gather his people (Mark 13:26-27); but until then, Christians will live a scattered life among the nations of this world, showing and speaking of how wonderful it is to be "a servant of God and of the Lord Jesus Christ" (James 1:1).

And as we read through James' letter, he will show us what solid, real, joyful faith looks like for scattered, suffering people.

Apply

- It's better to be a faithful servant of Jesus than a biological brother to him. What ways has he given you to serve him today?
- How are you finding life difficult at the moment as a scattered follower of God? How do you need to pray for God's help?

Bible in a year: 1 Kings 19 – 22

Joyful problems?!

Read James 1:2. Then read it again. And if it doesn't sound crazy, rub your eyes, get a coffee and read it again!

Pure joy

James says we can consider the many trials of our lives "pure joy"! He isn't wrong or lying—the Holy Spirit dictated what he wrote. So our God is saying we can find joy in the trials of life. Those are strange words, but words full of hope.

TIME OUT

❓ Why would it be wonderful to be able to consider the trials you face "pure joy"?

There is an idea that Christians won't suffer.

❓ How does verse 2 blow this out of the water?

James is going to spend his letter addressing the trials that test our faith in Christ. He will talk about suffering, doubt and also the surprising but no less serious trials of riches, power and success.

TIME OUT

❓ Today, which sort of trial could tug you away from Jesus?

❓ Which trial have you seen do the most damage to Christians you have known (maybe yourself)?

The normal grind of life and the lure of approval from others are more damaging of my trust in Jesus than the suffering I have faced. For others it is the opposite. I need to recognise my trials; and be joyful.

Because...

Read James 1:3-4

❓ What does the testing of our faith lead to (v 3-4)?

This "steadfastness" (v 3, ESV) isn't an end in itself. It's not about having a stiff upper lip. It's about keeping going in our faith. It's about experiencing a deep-down joy that simply comes from knowing and serving Jesus today, and knowing that we'll be with him one day (see v 12).

It's about facing the hardest times of our lives and saying, "However awful this trial is, I will still have Jesus. I can still serve Jesus. I will still be with Jesus. And this trial will make me more like Jesus, more mature and complete. It's better to go through this trial than not to."

If we manage to do that, we'll know pure joy! But this attitude doesn't come naturally to me or to many of us! We need to ask God to give it to us.

Pray

Bring your trials before your loving Father and trust that he's working through them.

Tell him how you are instinctively feeling about your trials. Ask the Lord to help you know and meditate on the "pure joy" of knowing his Son. Ask him to mature you as his child through the difficulties you face.

Bible in a year: Psalm 75 – 77

Wise faith

James wants to help scattered Christians face trials with joy. Can this really be our experience right now, today?

Faithful or doubting?
Read James 1:5

Pray

This is a very clear, simple and wonderful promise. Why not ask our Father for such wisdom now?

Read James 1:6-8

This seems to undo the generosity of verse 5!

- What does James describe as the opposite of believing (v 6)?
- What is the result of this (v 7)?
- What kind of person is James outlining (v 8)?

We need to see with crystal clarity what James means here. Doubt here is opposed to faith. It is the opposite, so that the one who doubts is "double-minded"—torn between a life of faith and a life of doubt. Doubt here is deliberately, rebelliously not fully trusting Jesus—and so not really trusting him at all.

If you sometimes experience doubts, but long to have those doubts replaced by certainty in Christ, you are not the person in James's sights.

TIME OUT
Read Mark 9:14-29

This man seems "double-minded". But when he asks Jesus for help (or in James's terms, prays for wisdom) he's answered.

- What is the difference here compared to someone who is truly "double-minded" (v 24 is crucial)?

Apply

Honestly consider your doubts (if you have, or have ever had, them).

- Do you long to trust Christ more or are you wilfully playing devil's advocate against Jesus and against placing unreserved faith in him?

Humbled and exalted

James wants us to see ourselves in terms of our relationship with God, not our circumstances. That includes our wealth.

Read James 1:9-11

- What is the "high position" every Christian enjoys (look back to v 1)? How will this lift up (or "exalt") a poor Christian?
- What does the rich Christian need to remember? How will this keep them humble?

Apply

- What tempts you to doubt Jesus' goodness? What steps will you take to respond to these tests with faith?
- Whether rich or poor, how will your faith impact how joyful you are, and where your joy comes from, today?

Bible in a year: Proverbs 7

Your crown of life

James wants us to stand firm through all the trials of life in this world because he knows a lot is at stake.

Read James 1:12

- ❓ What will God give to those who persevere in the face of trials?
- ❓ How does this motivate us to keep going in hard times?
- ❓ How will this enable us to consider trials "pure joy"?

A great future lies in store for those who trust Jesus to the end. James wants to help us be those people! And he does so by telling us to do two things.

Know the nature of temptation

Read James 1:13-15

- ❓ What is not happening when you are tempted to sin?
- ❓ Where does temptation to sin come from (v 14)?
- ❓ Why is it vital to take temptation seriously (v 15)?

Our desires motivate us, and so tempt us. For instance, I desire to be popular, so I flatter people and end up denying Christ because I care too much about my friends' opinions. Sin kills our love for and relationship with God, and ultimately leads to eternal death in hell instead of the crown of life with him.

Know God's character

Read James 1:16-18

Temptation is our desires telling us that we know what brings us joy—that the best life lies in following our feelings.

- ❓ What does James say to that (v 16)?
- ❓ How will believing verse 17 destroy the power of our desires over us?

We are the firstfruits of God's new creation (v 18). The firstfruits were the first part of the harvest, that spoke of even more to come.

This means that we can know victory now, by turning away from ourselves and looking to the Father of lights to see the gifts he gives us. And we can know that ultimate victory is guaranteed us, not because of how good we are, but because of who God is—our unchanging, gift-giving, life-promising Father.

🔼 Pray

Thank God for who he is. Ask him for wisdom to recognise and resist the temptation of following your desires.

🔽 Apply

- ❓ What temptations will you face today? How will your desires seek to deceive you today?
- ❓ When will you most need to remember to obey your Father God to enjoy goodness in life, rather than following your feelings?

Bible in a year: Ezekiel 13 – 18

James 1:19-25 — Saturday 5 July

Listen, but don't just listen

Rage flares up in a moment and I snap at my colleague, wife or daughter and shake my fist at the other driver. Afterwards it's so easy to parade the excuses.

Sound familiar? It can seem inevitable. But how often have you lost your rag with someone after listening carefully to them? How about after listening to God?

Shhhh…

Read James 1:19-21

- What three things does James tell his "dear brothers" to be?
- How do we avoid getting angry?
- Why is not getting angry important for Christians (v 20)?
- What two things will enable us to live this kind of life (v 21)?

Apply

- When in life do you most need to pause and remember verses 19-20?

Don't merely listen

In the Bible, the "word" refers to both the message about Jesus and to Jesus himself. We need to bear both in mind as we…

Read James 1:22-25

- If we come to the word only to listen, what do we achieve?
- What further step do we need to take?
- Why do you normally look in a mirror? What do you do afterwards if you notice your hair is a disaster zone?!

- So, what use is listening to the Bible, and then not acting on what we've read?

Verse 25 tells us to look into the "law"—which may not sound like a fun read…

- But what two things will it give us, if we read and follow it?

Freedom from our emotions being directed by circumstances. Joy in the middle of trials. Defining ourselves not by our wealth but by our status as God's children. The blessing of eternal life. Peace instead of anger. Living the life we were designed for. This is what James has already offered us, just in chapter 1! The question is: will we read God's word, close it and forget it—or will we read it, believe it and live it?

Apply

The challenge of James 1:22 is the reason why there are *Apply* sections like this one!

- Are there any ways that you currently know what God's word says but refuse to live by it?
- How does verse 25 encourage you to change?
- What could you do to make sure you remember the Bible passage Explore points you to each day? What could you do to make sure you "do what it says" (the Bible, not Explore!)?

Bible in a year: Luke 15 – 16

Just deserts

It says something about David's life that we have no idea what episode this psalm refers to. Fleeing from enemies who wanted him dead was his "normal"!

Caught in the crosshairs

Read Psalm 64:1-6

Sometimes we read of David being chased or attacked. Here, he is the target of plots, schemes and plans.

- ❓ What do we learn about those conspiring to destroy him?
- ❓ Why are they not afraid to oppose God's anointed king?

An eye for an eye

Read Psalm 64:7-10

- ❓ How is God's justice described in verses 7-8?
- ❓ How does it link back to verses 1-6?

In other words, what is being described here is *perfect justice*. David's enemies are getting exactly what they deserve. The things that they sought to do to David will be done to them. This is not revenge. Nor does God just ignore what has been done. This is justice.

- ❓ What impact will God's justice have on other people (v 9-10)?

This is a common theme in the Psalms. When people see justice being done, they fear God and turn away from evil. As Isaiah 26:9 puts it, "When your judgments come upon the earth, the people of the world learn righteousness". Likewise God's people are filled with praise.

TIME OUT

As we read about the life of Jesus in the Gospels, we see this psalm played out on a far greater stage. After Jesus' final arrival in Jerusalem a few days before his death, all the Gospels record the religious leaders plotting his death. They lay traps for him and seek to catch him out in their arguments (see Luke 19:47-48; 20:20; 22:1-6). One can imagine Jesus drawing strength as he prayed through this psalm and took refuge in the Lord, confident that God his Father would one day bring justice.

˅ Apply

- ❓ How might knowing that God will bring justice help someone who is suffering at the hands of other people today, and who is struggling not to give in to bitterness and a desire for vengeance?

˄ Pray

Praise God that he is the God of justice.

Ask that when you face injustice, you would be able to pray and trust God, rather than becoming angry and seeking revenge.

Pray for those suffering terrible injustice now, that they would be comforted by the example of the Lord Jesus, and the words of psalms like this that promise God's justice.

Bible in a year: Philippians 3 – 4

No mouth, all trousers

James has been talking about how we need to listen to the word—and then we need to do what it says. He's continuing with the same theme here.

Open mouth, closed heart

Read James 1:26

❓ *Why is this verse a challenge to all of us?*

What we do with our tongues, and what it shows about us, is a theme James will return to in chapter 3.

--- TIME OUT ---

Read Luke 12:1-3

Jesus was often at loggerheads with those who considered themselves religious.

❓ *How do his words here reinforce James 1:26?*

A friend of mine talks about being "all mouth and no trousers". It's possible to be like this when it comes to our religious life—and it's deadly. We con ourselves, we feel religious, proud of our faith. This kind of religion is unattractive to others, and it's unattractive to God.

🔺 Pray

Thank God that he can see, and that he dislikes, religious hypocrisy. Ask him to help you see whether there is any danger of you falling into this trap.

Closed mouth, open heart

I feel pretty bruised by James 1:26! But James has some good news for us.

Read James 1:27

The alternative to a closed heart and flapping tongue is to shut my mouth and open my heart. That is what verse 27 is—an invitation to a life of love and faith.

We're used to thinking about only loving our family and our friends.

❓ *But how does James challenge us to have a more radical love in verse 27?*

We find it easy(ish!) to feel full of joy and purity in church on Sundays, but...

❓ *... how does James challenge us to worship more radically in verse 27?*

🔽 Apply

❓ *What does it look like for you to care for the needy and vulnerable in your church and your community?*

❓ *In what ways could you pray this week to be freed from the pollution of a rebellious world?*

Remember that great promise in verse 5. If working out how to live verse 27 feels daunting, then go back there—it is a verse I have come to know backwards!

Bible in a year: Leviticus 10 – 12

Tuesday 8 July — James 2:1-7

Welcome to our church(?)

By now, you'll be used to the fact that James's letter is never less than challenging! And it is again today—a huge challenge, followed by a wonderful truth.

- In our culture, where are you welcomed if you have money? Where are you welcomed if you are poor?
- What about our churches?

Sometimes the way we welcome people in our churches is the same as everywhere else in society—money and appearance talk. This is a huge problem in sharing our faith with the poor; and an even bigger problem for our own hearts.

Read James 2:1

- How does James describe his readers?

Pray

Thank God that you have a glorious King, Jesus. Thank him that because you believe in him, you are part of his family, with brothers and sisters all over the world.

Free from discriminating

Read James 2:1-4

- When you came to Jesus, which of the two descriptions in verse 2 were you more like?
- Have you ever acted (or felt) like the imaginary church member James "quotes" in verse 3?
- When we discriminate, what do we become?

If we judge, we don't only wrong those we are discriminating against: we also wrong Jesus. He is the true Judge.

Apply

It's easy to act in a verse-3 way without even noticing!

- What are the ways in which your church could fall into this trap?
- In those situations, what would showing no favouritism look like?

Free from discrimination

Read James 2:5-7

- Why is verse 5 brilliant (especially if we're not particularly impressive in worldly terms)?
- How did the rich and influential people treat Christians (v 6-7)?

This is how they treated Christ—despite the truth that he is eternally glorious (v 1)!

- So why was it odd for James's readers to seek favour with these groups?

Apply

- Are there people you are in the habit (perhaps currently unnoticed) of looking down on? How will you use verse 5 to change your heart attitudes?

Pray

Thank God that he doesn't have favourites! Thank him for making you more welcoming of others since you became a Christian.

Bible in a year: 2 Kings 1 – 5

A royal pardon

Kings make laws, and good kings make good laws. Subjects need to obey the laws, and it's a bad subject who breaks a good law.

A great law

Read James 2:8

- What is the "royal law"?

Read Matthew 22:35-40

- How does this help us understand why James describes this law as "royal"?
- Why is this law a good law?

A great crime

This is the highest law the Creator King gives about how we are to treat others.

Read James 2:9-11

- How does showing favouritism break this law?
- I cringe to think of the ways I show favouritism—what about you?
- So what does the law declare us to be (v 9)?

James makes the point that even if I only break one part of the law, I am still a law-breaker. It is a royal law, given by Christ—so to break it is to reject the good and loving rule of King Jesus.

TIME OUT

God's law is like a pane of glass. Breaking it in one place shatters all of it. So we can't think that not murdering, stealing or defrauding means that our lying or envy or favouritism doesn't matter!

Pray

Reread verse 10 and use it to admit to God the ways in which you've broken his royal law this week.

A great mercy

We are guilty of despising King Jesus by breaking his law. We'd expect the punishment for a terrible act of rebellion to be severe.

Read James 2:12-13

Verse 12 talks of a law that will free us when we are judged by it. This can't be the royal law, because we've broken that!

Read Colossians 2:13-14

- Where does Jesus deal with our law-breaking, so that we can be forgiven and receive mercy?

This law takes us to Jesus, whose mercy triumphs over the judgment we deserve. He is the one who suffered our punishment so that we can be judged by a "perfect" law of mercy, instead of by the law we have broken.

Apply

Thank King Jesus for being your Saviour!

- James 2:12-13 reminds us that if we have truly received mercy from the King, we will show it to others. How can you do that this week?

Bible in a year: Psalm 78 – 80

A faith which works

"Whoever believes in the Son has eternal life" (John 3:36). "Righteousness is given through faith in Jesus Christ to all who believe" (Romans 3:22).

And then there's James 2…

Read James 2:14

- What is the shock here?
- All of Scripture is written by God (2 Timothy 3:16). So how do you and I fit this verse with the two truths from John and Romans above?

Lying faith

Read James 2:15-16

Picture the scene: a friend in church has no money and asks for help. My wallet is full and my bank balance healthy, and I answer, "I love you, and I'll pray for you". And I keep my wallet firmly closed.

- What does that show about my words?

Faith is trust. The reason we put our faith in Jesus is because he's shown himself to be faithful to us. In living a perfect life, in dying our death, in rising to give us new life, in sitting at God's right hand and speaking for us as his brothers, he is completely dependable. We trust him because he is utterly trustworthy.

If I *say* I trust you but refuse to lend you £10, I don't *really* trust you. The reality of my trust is shown through how I act in different circumstances. I can have faith before I've done anything at all—but what I do will show that I have that faith.

Dead faith

Read James 2:17-19

- What is "faith" if it never leads to action (v 17)?
- The hypothetical challenge in verse 18 tries to split works and faith. What does James do in his reply?
- Is a faith which doesn't lead to works any use? Is what we do any use on its own?

James is showing us that "faith" we refuse to act on isn't real, trusting faith—it is mere intellectual understanding. If I say I believe that you are trustworthy, but I don't lend you the tenner, I don't actually trust you.

- What do the demons believe about God in verse 19?

And they're right to acknowledge this! But they don't trust in Jesus as their Lord and Saviour. And that's seen in what they do—they work against Jesus, rather than living under his rule.

Martin Luther, the 16th-century Reformer, put it very helpfully: "We are saved by faith alone, but the faith that saves is never alone".

Pray

Thank God for saving you. Thank him for giving you faith. Thank him for the opportunities he gives you in life to show your living faith through what you do.

Bible in a year: Proverbs 8 – 9

Faith alone?

James 2 takes us to the heart of one of the greatest splits in the institutional church.

The issue

The medieval Catholic church taught that faith is the beginning of our salvation. Salvation must then be completed by our good works. The Protestant Reformers, like Luther and John Calvin, taught that we are justified (declared righteous by God) by faith alone.

Read James 2:20-26

- *How does the example James gives in verses 21-23 seem to support the Catholic view?*

The example

James is taking us back to the life of Abram (later renamed Abraham), the father of the nation of Israel. The crucial thing in understanding James is to realise that James talks about an event in verses 21-22 that happens in Genesis 22, and yet in James 2:23 he quotes from Genesis 15, from an event which happened years earlier.

Read Genesis 15:1-6

- *What is Abram's problem (v 1-3)?*
- *What does God promise (v 3-4)?*
- *What does faith look like at this point (v 6)?*
- *How does God respond to Abram's faith (v 6)?*

Abram's real faith means he simply believes God's promise. He does nothing. And God says at this point that he is righteous.

Later (Genesis 22:1-2) the Lord told Abraham to sacrifice that promised son (and then gave a ram to take his place).

- *At the point when God tells Abraham to sacrifice Isaac, what would trusting faith look like?*

And that's what Abraham did, says James (James 2:21). "His faith and his actions were working together" (v 22). The reality of his faith was shown in what he did. If he'd refused to trust God with his son's life, it would have shown that he didn't have real, righteous-making faith at all.

It is not that God sees true faith, in Abraham or in us, and then waits for us to do good works before declaring us right with him, justified. God responds to true faith by making us righteous; and then his verdict on that faith—as being true and alive—is shown publicly, or "fulfilled" (v 23), by the way that our faith affects how we act.

Apply

Real trust in Jesus affects all we do.

- *Think through your day. How will real faith affect what you do?*
- *How would you answer someone who says that these verses show we're saved by faith and good deeds?*

Bible in a year: Ezekiel 19 – 24

Saturday 12 July — James 3:1-12

Taming a teacher's tongue

This is a passage that mainly has teachers like me in its sights!

The humbled teacher

Read James 3:1-2

Most of the letter is addressed to "you". These verses use "we" instead. James humbly puts himself in the same position as other teachers.

- ❓ Why is it a daunting responsibility to be a Bible teacher (v 1)?
- ❓ So why might the beginning of verse 2 be very worrying for Christian teachers?
- ❓ How does 2:12 free them to open their mouths at all?

The dangerous tongue

Read James 3:3-7

If I were in a fight, I wouldn't be that worried about the other guy's tongue but his fists! Yet James wants us to see that in many ways, the tongue is the most powerful and dangerous part of the body.

- ❓ Why (v 5-6)?
- ❓ What is the main point of verses 3-8?
- ❓ Do verses 7-8 give any hope of making ourselves great teachers?

The double-tongued Christian

In 1:8, James introduced us to the idea of the double-minded person. This is someone who is half-trying to live as a Christian but also trying to live with themselves and their desires in charge. It is a miserable double-life, full of tension and compromise.

Read James 3:8-12

James seems to be starting to talk to the whole church again—his "brothers" (v 10).

- ❓ What two things do Christians do with their tongues (v 9)?
- ❓ What's the answer to the questions in verses 11-12?

▼ Apply

- ❓ How and when does verse 9 ring true of you? What needs to change?

▲ Pray

The problem is, on my own I can't change (v 8)! So we need to head back to 1:5—to ask God for his wisdom and to give us tongues which only praise him and do not curse.

Why not pray now for God's wisdom:

- to direct how you use your words today.
- to show you where you're using your tongue to complain about or criticise or curse his creatures.
- to enable you to see how you might use your tongue to point people to Jesus.

Then pray for the teachers in your church—that they will praise our Lord in all they say, and not start hellish fires.

Bible in a year: Luke 17 – 18

Thanksgiving

How thankful are you? I'm a world-class grumbler, and this psalm is a great rebuke and reminder to me to work at thankfulness!

Context

It's no wonder that this psalm is so thankful after Psalms 51 – 64. David has been through seemingly unforgivable sin, deadly plots, relentless pursuit from enemies and exile far away from the presence of God. Now God has delivered him from all those threats, he is bound to be rather full of praise!

Sins forgiven

Read Psalm 65:1-4

David begins by praising God for forgiveness. (Do you remember how he desperately cried out for it in Psalm 51?)

> ❓ What does forgiveness make possible, according to Psalm 65:4?

God is no longer found in one particular place (John 4:20-24), but the greatest thing about coming to him for forgiveness is the same for us—it's not that our guilt is gone, as good as that is; it is that we can now have a relationship of love and intimacy with the living God.

Secure hope

Read Psalm 65:5-8

> ❓ What do we learn about God?
> ❓ Hope is focused on things we don't yet have. What do we look forward to as Christians?
> ❓ What gives us confidence that God will do what he has promised?

Abundant supply

Read Psalm 65:9-13

The final verses are full of praise to God for how he provides for us. If you are a farmer, I guess they'd be wonderfully moving. However, we tend to get our food from the supermarket, not the ground, so we may need to put verses 9-13 into modern language:

You care for the economy and visit it with growth, you enrich it abundantly.
The banks of God are filled with funds to provide the people with rent, food, wine, even artisan coffee and iPhones.

You raise taxes to pay for teachers and doctors, you provide security and rule of law so that people invest in this country and grow businesses here. The money in our banks is safe, guaranteed by the government.

You crown the year with your bonuses, and your supermarkets overflow with fresh, tasty produce from all around the world.

The shelves in the shops are full of luxuries as well as necessities, our houses have heating and running water and electricity, and televisions and washing machines and broadband–your goodness overflows!

⌄ Apply

> ❓ How do you think it would affect your attitude to others and your happiness if you started each day thanking God for all that he has given you?

Bible in a year: Colossians 1 – 2

Real wisdom

Who would you say is the wisest person in public life? David Attenborough? Oprah Winfrey? ChatGPT?! Who is the wisest person you know, if you needed help and advice?

Actually, what makes someone "wise"?! Here James shows us what a wise life looks like, and it is a challenge to me as someone who does love to talk!

Actions, not words

Read James 3:13-16

Real wisdom is seen not in what we say so much as what we do.

- *What is a wise person like?*
- *True wisdom produces real humility. What's the opposite to humility (v 14)?*
- *Where does this fake "wisdom" come from, and what does it lead to (v 15-16)?*

···· TIME OUT ····

We so often think of wisdom being about what we say, and we like the thought of being able to help people with our wise words.

If our desire to be wise is driven by wanting other people to think we're wise, it's likely that we're being described by verse 14! And there's no short-cut to being a wise adviser; first, we need to live a wise life. And that isn't easy!

Wisdom from heaven

Read James 3:17

- *What is the wisdom that is from heaven like?*
- *Pause to consider what each of the qualities in verse 17 actually means in real life.*
- *This is not a difficult question (hopefully!): does verse 14 or verse 17 sound better?*
- *How do you get this heavenly wisdom? (Our favourite, 1:5, will help!)*

Wise words

Read James 3:18

In the Bible the images of making peace between people and God, and of sowing, are related to telling people the good news of Jesus. That is what James has in mind here. The person of humble, godly wisdom is the person who seeks to speak the gospel of peace with God through Christ into people's lives.

···· TIME OUT ····

- *From these verses, how would you answer the question: "What is wisdom"?*

Pray

Again, ask God for his wisdom (1:5)!

- *Is there any particular aspect of James 3:14 that you need to ask God to help you get rid of in your heart?*
- *Is there any particular quality of verses 17-18 that you would like to ask God to grow in you?*

Bible in a year: Leviticus 13 – 15

James 4:1-3 — Tuesday 15 July

Just ask

James is writing to a real church, just like ours. And this real church, like all churches, knew its share of squabbling.

The manipulation issue

Read James 4:1-2

- What is the initial cause of human conflict (v 1)?
- How do people go about getting what they want (v 2—first three sentences in NIV1984 translation, first two sentences in NIV2011!)?

TIME OUT

- Have there been times when your own desires have led to quarrels... envy... manipulation... outright conflict?

We may not murder to get what we want. But I know there are times when, in order to achieve what I desire, I manipulate situations, and people. The end begins to justify the means. I do wrong things, telling myself that it's for the right reasons.

- Instead of working out how we can get what we want by ourselves, what should we do (end of verse 2)?

The motive issue

James has just told us that we don't have because we don't ask. But what about when we do ask, and don't get?!

Read James 4:3

- Why do we not get what we want, even when we pray for it (v 3)?

It's not wrong to desire things. It's not wrong to ask God for those things. But once we're speaking to the Father of the heavenly lights, the Lord of eternity, we'll begin to ask ourselves why. Why am I asking for a bigger car or a better kitchen? What are my motives—to be able to give an elderly church member a lift or get my children to where they need to be, to be more hospitable or teach my children how to cook... or because the neighbours have got a nicer car or new kitchen?

Prayer is simply a child of God asking their Father for a gift, so they can enjoy living with and for their Father. We just need to ask—amazing! But if our motive for asking is because we long to find pleasure elsewhere—in the gift, not the Giver—then "you do not receive" (v 3).

Apply

For each of these prayers, think about what would be some right motives for asking, and what could be some wrong motives.

"Our Father in heaven, please...
... give me a bigger house."
... let me love my co-workers better."
... use me to bring my friend to church."
... heal me."
... give me that promotion."
... make me a great preacher."
... fill me with your Spirit."

It's good always to keep in mind our motives because God cares more about our motives than our words.

Bible in a year: 2 Kings 6 – 10

My best friend is…?

If our attitude to the world is friendship, what is our attitude to God?

Sleeping with the enemy

Read James 4:4-6

There are at least three ways to read verse 5! I think it's best to translate "envies" as "longs jealously", and to understand "spirit" as the Holy Spirit (as the second option in the NIV footnote does).

❷ *How does the Spirit feel about our friendship with the world?*

His jealousy is well-founded. Jesus came to buy back his bride, the church, at the cost of his life. He gave us the Spirit to live in us. Then he sees us fooling around with the world he saved us from.

Friendship with the world is loving the things God made without loving them in relationship with him. I can enjoy a weekend take-away because I feel I've earned it. Or I can enjoy it as a gift from our Father, who gave me work, energy and rest—so many good gifts (1:17)!

Apply

In these situations, what would it look like to be friends with the world, and what would it look like to live as a child of God? The answers may not be simple!

- The neighbours get a great new car.
- You're offered a new job.
- If you move house, your child can go to a better school.
- Your friends discuss the gorgeous actor/actress in the latest hit drama.

More and more kindness

At this point we might expect God to remind us of what Jesus did for us and shame us into bucking up our attitude.

Read James 4:6-10

❷ *What does he do instead (v 6)?*
❷ *Why is this…*
  • *amazing?*
  • *encouraging?*
❷ *God gives this to the "humble" (v 6)—so what do we need to do (v 7-10a)?*
❷ *How does God respond to this kind of person (v 8, 10)?*

This is serious. But it isn't miserable. It's the way to find ourselves knowing a more intimate relationship with our Lord, being blessed by him, enjoying all his good gifts. We may not have the world, but we'll have Jesus—and there's nothing better than that!

Apply

❷ *What will this serious, grace-reliant humility look like for you today?*
❷ *Do you find it easy to believe that verses 7-10 are a better way to live or do you need to pray for help with this?*

Bible in a year: Psalm 81 – 83

James 4:11-17 — Thursday 17 July

Heavenly life

A good friend asked me the other day whether it was right to pray for more business for the company he works for. Good question!

❓ *What do you think?*

Good judgment

Read James 4:11-12

If you judge another Christian, you judge the law. James is thinking of the "law of mercy" that frees us (2:12-13). God has declared us righteous in Christ, so we have no place to judge each other.

❓ *I judge other Christians to make myself feel I am better than them as a follower of Jesus. What does James 4:11 convict me of doing?*

❓ *What does verse 12 say to me?*

▾ Apply

If I am shown mercy, this frees me from judging other Christians. I don't need to look down on others to feel good about myself. I can look up to Christ and see his welcome and feel good about him.

❓ *How will doing this change our attitude towards other Christians?*

❓ *Are there any particular ways this challenges you?*

Good business

We all like to make big plans. We all like to sound good. That's why you don't see many adverts saying: "Average products that probably won't change your life at a slightly above-average price". I don't often try to give the impression that I'm the mediocre preacher and so-so pastor that I really am. Projecting outward confidence isn't limited to ad executives!

Read James 4:13-17

❓ *What is the attitude behind verse 13?*

❓ *How does verse 14 show this to be foolish?*

❓ *What does this say about where our confidence lies, according to verse 16?*

❓ *What is the good we ought to do in verse 17? Look back to 1:27 for help.*

My friend's desire to see the company he works for flourish is good. If he prays for more business, and then trusts God to do what is best, he is living this passage. The alternative is to decide for himself what is best, and then seek it without God—and "all such boasting is evil".

Whether our "business" is a building site, church, company, home, school or whatever, we need to want Christ's will to triumph there more than we want our own plans to. And after all, we know that his plans are always better than ours, however well-laid!

Read Psalm 1:6; Proverbs 3:5-6; and/or Romans 8:28-29.

▴ Pray

What is the "business" of your day, week and year? Why not pray about it all and seek the Lord's will for it.

Bible in a year: Proverbs 10

What to do with wealth

This is one of those passages that is stunningly and immediately relevant to 21st-century Western culture.

The dangers of wealth 1

Our society is rich and loves richness. Whether you feel well off or not when you compare yourself to your friends, our culture is built on the simple idea that the cooler, bigger, faster and more expensive our stuff is, the happier our lives are.

Read James 5:1-3

- ❓ When we look at our riches, what should our response be (v 1)?
- ❓ What is the problem with wealth in verses 2-3?
- ❓ How does the last sentence of verse 3 make our behaviour worse?

When we hoard money and stuff, we are saying we trust it to save us. It promises status, comfort and security, so we make it more important than Jesus. I think I will always have a place to live because I have insured my house, and enjoy comfort because I have the latest gadget, not because my home is in heaven with Jesus and I will have heavenly riches with him.

The dangers of wealth 2

Read James 5:4-6

- ❓ How have the rich become rich? Who has paid the cost?
- ❓ Who is listening to the harvesters' cries?

Wealth is not always the result of exploiting others. But to grasp after wealth means I ignore others in my selfishness. Have people been exploited in order to give me the lifestyle I enjoy? If the answer is "yes", I need to be honest about whether these verses are targeted at me.

James doesn't say it's wrong to have wealth. It's what we do with it that counts. And it's very easy to find lots of apparently sensible reasons to do the wrong things with it.

TIME OUT

Read Luke 19:1-10

Notice that Zacchaeus ends this passage as a wealthy man, just as he started it.

- ❓ What has changed though?
- ❓ How does Zacchaeus show how to be a wealthy Christian?

▾ Apply

It's very hard simply to give up our wealth. Not just because our finance-based societies seem to lock us in, but because we love to have wealth! What we can do, though, is to replace it with a greater love.

- ❓ In who we rely on, how can we copy the harvesters of James 5:4?
- ❓ How can we copy Zacchaeus in what we love most?
- ❓ If you love and rely on Jesus instead of wealth, without seeking wiggle room, how will that affect the way your bank statement looks?

Bible in a year: Ezekiel 25 – 30

Have a little patience

We don't live in a patient age. Being patient seems a bit... boring!

The conclusion...
Read James 5:7-9

- *In what ways does the example of a farmer teach us about patience?*
- *How does the Christ-loving attitude of verses 7-8 contrast with the wealth-reliant one of yesterday's passage?*

We tend to think that to "stand firm" is about my personal commitment to Jesus.

- *How does verse 9 put my standing firm in relation to other Christians and to Jesus?*

It sounds as if we just need to keep our heads down, and Jesus will come soon. But it is more than this. Knowing Jesus is coming gives us the courage to stand firm as a united people until then. It gives us faith.

... but not the end
Read James 5:10-12

These verses show us what it looks like to be patient as we wait for the end.

- *Which group is our example of patience? What did they do?*

Job endured family tragedy, financial ruin, crippling illness and rubbish friends. He experienced the worst that we can possibly face.

- *What does the end of verse 11 suggest Job remembered about God? How would this have helped him to persevere?*

Apply

The outcome of Job's endurance was even greater blessing than at the beginning. The Lord shows us compassion and mercy during suffering and in the results of suffering.

- *What suffering is facing you now? Are there ways you can see the Lord's compassion and mercy even as you endure it?*
- *How could you keep reminding yourself that Jesus is with you now and is coming in glory soon, so that you endure patiently?*

Pray

We need huge help to suffer patiently, trusting Jesus. We have a Lord of compassion and mercy. I don't know what you're facing right now, but he does. He loves you deeply, and he will show you his compassion and mercy. You can trust his words here in James. He will not let you down.

So why not pray about the trials you or a Christian loved one are facing today.

Look back at your answers to the questions in *Apply*, and turn them into prayers.

Bible in a year: Luke 19 – 20

Take up your cross…

For some reason, the nicer the holiday, the worse the journey to get there. But it's worth it when you finally arrive and walk onto the soft, sandy beach…

This psalm has that sense of relief on arrival. God has rescued David and brought him through all his troubles.

All the world
Read Psalm 66:1-4

Throughout Psalms 42 – 64 the nations have attacked and opposed God's king, David. But David doesn't want the nations of the world bowing before him in miserable defeat; he wants them to bow before the Lord in delighted worship!

He saved Israel
Read Psalm 66:5-7

David recounts how God has treated Israel, so that the nations would learn how good God is and trust in him.

❓ *What incident in the life of Israel is David referring to?*

Christians don't look back to the exodus. We look back to what the exodus looked forward to—the death of Jesus on the cross which redeemed us not from slavery in Egypt but the much worse slavery to our sin and death.

He disciplined Israel
Read Psalm 66:8-12

❓ *According to verse 10, why were the hard times a good thing?*

❓ *Where was God leading his people (v 11)?*

So also me
Read Psalm 66:13-20

Now David reflects that God has dealt with him in a similar way. God is like that; his character is dependable, predictable and unchanging. David talks in verses 13-15 of offering sacrifices to God. In other words, when God has done good things for him, he wants to respond by praising God and by giving generously. In verses 16-20 he tells us what it is that God did.

▼ Apply

When Jesus says, "Take up [your] cross daily and follow me" (Luke 9:23), he's calling us to follow him on the road marked by self-denial and difficulty in this world, but it is the road that leads to eternal delight, glory and praise with God in paradise. As we walk on this road, praying for God's help, we know that he will rescue us and bring us safely home to be with him for ever.

▲ Pray

This psalm calls us to pray great big global prayers for the spread of the gospel. Why not pray for missionaries whom you know?

It also encourages us to pray for God's strength and rescue as we trust him through the trials of this life.

Bible in a year: Colossians 3 – 4

Ups, downs and sickness

I am an atheist. Or at least, I often live like one. The great news is, I don't need to!

TIME OUT

- ❓ When something goes wrong, how do you react in feelings and actions?
- ❓ When things are great and you're happy with life, what do you do?

Here's what I do. When things go wrong, I try to fix them or moan and grumble or blame someone. When life's full of happiness, I get on with enjoying it! God doesn't get much of a look-in. Which means I live like an atheist.

Dealing with ups and downs

Read James 5:13

- ❓ How does the Christian react to difficult times?
- ❓ How do they react to wonderful times?
- ❓ Who does the Christian relate to in suffering and cheerfulness?

An atheist lives in a world without God. A Christian lives all of life in relationship to God. This is the big idea of this short section, and it's wonderful. We can live all our life, in every season and emotion, in relationship with Jesus. Never alone!

▼ Apply

- ❓ How does this encourage you as a Christian today?
- ❓ How does it challenge you?

Dealing with sickness

Read James 5:14-15

We tend to see both sickness and prayer as private matters.

- ❓ How does verse 14 change our perspective?

Anointing (with oil, v 14) seems to be a symbol of the Holy Spirit (Isaiah 61:1).

- ❓ How will doing what James 5:14 says encourage a sick believer?
- ❓ Reread verse 15. What do you think James is promising that the elders' prayer will do?

This is tricky! The word translated "make ... well" here can also mean "save". "Raise them up" might refer to getting up from a sick bed; but it also has our ultimate resurrection, when Jesus returns, in view. So verse 15 is not a promise of earthly healing. (James knew, as we do, that Christians die.) God can heal, and may heal, and we pray for that when a loved one is ill. But God will save for eternity those who live and pray "in faith" (v 15).

The danger when sickness hits is not that we will suffer or even die. It is that we will abandon Christ in our suffering. So when we're ill it's great, and vital, to be ill Christians. We get others to pray for us; and we trust that God can and might heal us now, and that he will raise us up one day. **Read 1 Thessalonians 4:13-18.**

Bible in a year: Leviticus 16 – 18

Tuesday 22 July — James 5:15-18

Powerful prayer

James is continuing to tell us how to live the everyday, ordinary Christian life. And actually, it's pretty extraordinary!.

Dealing with sin

Read James 5:15-16a

❷ *What are Christians to do for one another (v 16)?*

Remember, "healed" (v 16) also means "saved". And we don't have to confess our sins to everyone—though a church where people can be honest about sin and pray for one another is a church of people who keep going in faith.

There is a connection between sin and sickness in the Bible, but we need to be careful. If we are ill, God is not punishing us: Christ has taken the penalty for all our sins. But God may be disciplining us; possibly to make us confront and confess a sin we've been ignoring or perhaps to give us more time to pray or to remind us that this world is painful and passing, and that eternity with God is far better.

So if we fall ill, we mustn't assume there is no link between our illness and our sin; but equally, we mustn't assume that there must be a link. The right question to ask is simply: what might God be teaching me through this trial? And the right response is: since God is working through this, I can have pure joy (1:2)!

And, as we saw yesterday, whatever struggles we have with sin or sickness, we have a powerful weapon.

Pray!

Read James 5:16b-18

❷ *What does James say a righteous man's prayer is (v 16)? How is this encouraging?*

❷ *What sort of man was Elijah (v 17)? Why do you think James describes him like this?*

❷ *What did he do, and what happened (v 17-18)?*

The story of Elijah's powerful prayers is in 1 Kings 17 – 18. It is well worth reading! Elijah was *like us*. And his prayers saw powerful answers. Righteous people can expect powerful answers to their prayers. Elijah was a righteous person—like us.

--- TIME OUT ---

Read 2 Corinthians 5:21

❷ *How are people like us made righteous, i.e. totally right with God?*

This is an amazing thing—Jesus has given his people, including Elijah and including us, his own righteousness. When Jesus died he took our sin, and he gave us his own perfect goodness. So when we Christians pray, we are as righteous as Jesus. Wow!

▲ Pray

❷ *How do these verses encourage you to pray more and for more? Let's pray!*

Bible in a year: 2 Kings 11 – 15

Launch the lifeboat

During the First World War, a lifeboat was launched off the Norfolk coast to help a ship sinking in a storm.

That's heroic—what is more remarkable was that the sinking ship had a German name. These ordinary, unpaid men rowed out to rescue their enemies. How much more will Christians want to man the oars for their brother or sister who is floundering?

Danger of drowning

James has told us how to face trials with joy, to pray for wisdom and to act on our faith. But what if we don't do this? What if our Christian friends don't? What if the sickness seems too bad, the suffering too great, the sin too overwhelming?

Read James 5:19-20

- How does James describe what can happen to a Christian?

TIME OUT

- What sort of "truth" about God or ourselves, do we tend to wander from when faced with…
  - suffering?
  - sin?
  - wealth?
  - poverty?

Mounting the rescue

- Who should struggling Christians be able to rely on?

In other words, all of us are to have the heart of the father in Jesus' parable of the two sons in Luke 15. Rescuing drowning Christians is not a job simply for pastors or small-group leaders or family members—it's a job for us. It sounds like hard work, though, to bring back a wandering brother or sister—after all, they have got themselves into trouble, and they might not welcome our attempts.

So in James 5:20, we are told what we achieve if we bring back a wandering sinner.

- What is that?
- Who saves souls from death and covers over sins? What is verse 20 saying is our role in this?
- How do these verses invite us to a mission as heroic and honourable as that of a lifeboat crew?

If we bring back to Jesus a Christian who is floundering, then we act like Jesus. He includes us in the work he is doing to save and care for his church. What a wonderful honour that is—to be like Christ to a friend who needs his help.

Apply

- Who do you know who is struggling? Who hasn't been to church for ages? Who's been ensnared by a sin?
- How could you pray for them?
- What truth about Jesus do they need you to remind them of? When will you speak to them about it?

Maybe you feel you are wandering yourself. Who could help you? Ask them! You'll be giving them a chance to be like Jesus.

Bible in a year: Psalm 84 – 86

Thursday 24 July — James (various)

Joy with Jesus

We have finished James! Today, we're looking back at the great themes of this wonderful, and extremely challenging, part of God's word.

You and I and the other *Explore* readers are scattered from each other like James's first readers (1:1). But like them, we are bound to one another by the Holy Spirit as God's "tribes", servants of the Lord Jesus (v 1).

Trials and temptations

Read James 1:2-5

- What is the great challenge of verse 2?
- What trials have you faced as you've studied James?
- In what ways has Jesus helped you to count it all joy when you meet trials, through reading this letter?
- In what ways have you gained wisdom, and seen how Jesus works more clearly, as you've read James?

James has engaged with lots of different trials that face us—illness, suffering, temptation to sin, favouritism, wealth, poverty, complacent faith, the tongue, self-confidence, boasting and more. If we looked at the trials, we would be lost—they would overwhelm us.

- Look at James 1:12, 17. Where should we look instead?

Where do you tend to look when troubles come? At the trial, in its bleakness or at your Father in his loving generosity? At the difficulty, in all its pain, or at the crown your Father stands ready to give you beyond it?

⌄ Apply

- Think about how you can look to our Father in the normal circumstances of life, day by day. What can you do to keep your eyes on him?

⌃ Pray

Talk to God about the trials you face. Ask him to surprise you with joyfulness as you walk through them.

Today and tomorrow

As James writes, he lifts our eyes to our God and Father. And he brings in more and more of a future perspective.

Read James 4:13-14

- How does our lack of knowledge about the future humble us?

Read James 5:7-8

- How does our certain knowledge about the future encourage and strengthen us?

⌃ Pray

I'm always humbled when I read James. He makes me so grateful for the Lord Jesus' forgiveness, and shows me so many ways I need to change.

Pick your greatest encouragement and challenge from our time in James, and talk to our Father about them now.

Bible in a year: Proverbs 11 – 12

Nehemiah 1:1-3 — Friday 25 July

NEHEMIAH: Meet the man

Recall your first day at a new school, a new job or a new church. You probably experienced information overload with new names and faces, right?

Here at the beginning of Nehemiah, we're given lots of new information in just three verses. Let's get the situation of this book in our heads.

Read Nehemiah 1:1-3

Verse 1 establishes that Nehemiah is the author. Most of the book will be told in his own words (though chapters 8 – 11 are narrated in the third person).

These verses assume that the reader has some basic knowledge of Israel's history leading up to the situation in which Nehemiah finds himself. Our own knowledge of this history may be rusty, so let's review five important background facts:

1. Over the course of its history, Israel had been divided into a northern kingdom (Israel) and a southern kingdom (Judah).

2. In 587 BC, the southern kingdom of Judah fell to Babylon, and the people were taken into exile, far from their homeland.

3. In 539 BC, Babylon itself was conquered by the kingdom of Persia.

4. Under the Persian kings, several groups of Jewish exiles returned home. The first group returned in 538 BC. Sixty years later, Ezra led another group. Nehemiah led the third wave.

5. At the beginning of this book, Nehemiah is in Persia—in "the citadel of Susa" (v 1)—far from home.

- *How does this background help explain why Nehemiah asks the questions he does when Hanani comes to town?*
- *What answer do the visiting Jews give to Nehemiah's questions (v 3)?*

The things mentioned in verse 3 will be key themes throughout the rest of this book.

- *Imagine being far from beloved relatives and hearing they're in danger. How would you feel? How would you respond?*

We've seen already in these first three verses of the book that Nehemiah faces a serious situation. In the studies to come, we'll see how a man of faith and action responds.

Pray

Ask God to teach and encourage you through your study of Nehemiah in the coming days.

Apply

Notice that Nehemiah is keen to find out about his fellow Jews—God's people—and about the state of his homeland—God's land.

- *How keen are you to keep up to date with the lives of fellow members of God's people, both near and far?*
- *How does, or could, this show itself in your life?*

Bible in a year: Ezekiel 31 – 36

A man who trusts

You can learn a lot about a person by hearing them pray. We have the privilege of overhearing many of Nehemiah's prayers in this book. Here's the first one.

Let's see what kind of a man Nehemiah is.

The reaction

Read Nehemiah 1:4

Nehemiah has just heard that God's people are in trouble, and that God's city of Jerusalem is in ruins.

- ❓ How does he respond?
- ❓ What does the fact that he prays tell us about what he sees as the cause of Israel's plight?

---- TIME OUT ----

Fasting is something few of us do, and we may not understand its significance.

Read 2 Samuel 1:11-12; 3:31-35

- ❓ Why did David fast?

Leviticus 16:29-31 calls for fasting on the Day of Atonement, the day on which the high priest made an offering for the sins of Israel.

- ❓ How does the background of these two passages help us understand why Nehemiah fasts?

The request

Read Nehemiah 1:5-10

- ❓ How does Nehemiah describe God (v 5)?
- ❓ Given what he has been showing through his fasting, why is Nehemiah's choice of description here important?
- ❓ What does he ask God for (v 6)?

Notice that Nehemiah humbly includes himself and his family among those who have sinned (v 6). It's much easier to name the sins of others than to admit our own sin, isn't it?

🔼 Pray

- ❓ Is there anything you need to confess now?

Now (v 8-9), Nehemiah asks God to keep his covenant promises to forgive and restore his people when they return to him (e.g. Deuteronomy 30:1-4).

The resolve

Read Nehemiah 1:11

- ❓ What does Nehemiah ask for here?
- ❓ What do we find out about Nehemiah in verse 11?

Nehemiah's job means he has some influence. And he's about to ask a huge favour of the king of Persia. After praying, Nehemiah takes action.

🔽 Apply

I realised a while back that I would pray for people, but not think how I might be the way God could answer my prayers.

- ❓ What are you praying for, for others? How could you take action as well as pray?

Bible in a year: Luke 21 – 22

Joy to the world

Knowing God's steadfast love makes us sing, and makes us long that both we and the world would know this love more.

Read Psalm 67

> ❓ Are you enjoying God's love, or has it become an insurance policy to look at on a tough day or even just an idea? If so, what will you do about that?

Heart singing

Back in the book of Numbers, God gave the priests a blessing to share with the people, recorded in Numbers 6:23-27. That is the blessing which opens the psalm. It's a deeply moving prayer. Worshipping hearts want nothing more, and need nothing less.

Reread Psalm 67:1. Worshipping hearts turn to God as praying hearts. We need to fight our naturally proud and independent spirits, and learn to rely on God, and want a rich experience of his grace. We need to humble ourselves to pray.

Apply

> ❓ What do you most want to shine on you? Success; health; wealth; or the face of God in Christ Jesus?

"Seek and you will find" (Matthew 7:7) is an invitation, never a burden!

> ❓ Are you joyfully seeking God's blessings at the moment?

Peace, perfect peace

As Christians, we can be at rest: God's face is always turned towards us in love. Because Jesus died and rose for us, paying the cost our sins deserve and guaranteeing us a new life, we can have even more conviction that God will bless us and keep us than his Old Testament people did. Hallelujah!

The great commission

Charles Wesley could have been reflecting on this psalm when he wrote these hymn words: "O that the world might taste and see the riches of his grace; the arms of love that compass me would all mankind embrace."

The writer of the psalm is praying for God's blessings to rest on his people. After all, didn't God tell their forefather Abraham that he would bless him and his offspring (see Genesis 12:2)—and also, the whole world (v 3)?

> ❓ Read Galatians 3:16. How does God's blessing come to the world?
>
> ❓ Now look at Matthew 28:16-20. What is the blessing God has for the world?
>
> ❓ What is our role in ensuring that the prayer of Psalm 67:3-5 becomes a reality?

Pray

Pray for the gospel-needy nations of the world. Pray that God would use you in cross-cultural mission, through prayer, finance and action, whether that be on your street or across the world.

Bible in a year: 1 Thessalonians 1 – 3

A man who acts

We learn a lot about a person by seeing what they're willing to do even when they're afraid. As we read this passage, imagine Nehemiah's heart in his throat!

Making the chance

Read Nehemiah 2:1-2

Nehemiah was the king's "cupbearer" (1:11). He chose wine for the Persian king, and tasted it to ensure that it was not poisoned. This position gave him significant access to the king. It's the king's favour that Nehemiah knows he needs, and has prayed for. He will need permission to speak; and then permission to act.

- How does God begin to answer Nehemiah's prayer in these verses?
- How does he feel?
- Will Nehemiah manage to speak?!

Read Nehemiah 2:3-4

- What subject does he immediately introduce?
- When the king asks him to present his request, what does Nehemiah do?

This is often called an "arrow" prayer—it's much shorter than the one in 1:5-11! It's shot up in a quick breath immediately before Nehemiah presents his request. Nehemiah is truly a man of prayer and courage, of faith and action!

- How does Nehemiah describe God in 2:4?
- How would it have helped him to remember this truth as he stood before the king?

Apply

When confronted with a difficult situation, how do you respond? Do you fall on the "action alone" end of the spectrum, throwing yourself immediately into problem-solving mode and forgetting to pray? Or are you on the "prayer alone" end of the spectrum, praying a lot about the situation but not really doing anything?

- How can you learn from Nehemiah?

Taking the chance

Read Nehemiah 2:5-8

- How does Nehemiah present his request in a way designed to make the king listen?
- What does he ask for (v 5, 7-8)?

Nehemiah demonstrates remarkable wisdom. His requests to the king are clear, direct, honest and humble. He has clearly given careful thought to what he wants to do to help his people.

- What is the outcome (v 8)?

Nehemiah doesn't take personal credit. Nor does he give the credit to the king for listening fairly and openly. Nehemiah knows who is the ultimate decision-maker in all of this.

Apply

- When, and for what things, are you most tempted to take the credit, instead of giving it to God?

Bible in a year: Leviticus 19 – 21

Going public

It seems Nehemiah's pulse has just stopped racing from his audience with the king, when it's time to go public with his plan. How will Israel and their enemies respond?

The opposition begins
Read Nehemiah 2:9-10

We're introduced here to two characters who will feature heavily in the rest of the book: Sanballat and Tobiah. In verse 19, we'll meet a third enemy. Notice how each man is identified: Sanballat the Horonite, Tobiah the Ammonite official, Geshem the Arab. These are members of nations who have been enemies of Israel for centuries.

❓ *How do they react to Nehemiah's plan?*

City tour
Read Nehemiah 2:11-16

❓ *What does verse 12 tell us about where Nehemiah's passion to rebuild Jerusalem comes from?*

❓ *What does Nehemiah discover on his tour of the capital city of God's land (v 12-15)?*

There must be tears on Nehemiah's cheeks and prayers on his lips as he rides through the night.

So far, the Jews themselves have no idea what Nehemiah is planning (v 12, 16). But it will be they who have to do the work. So Nehemiah needs to go public…

Let us start
Read Nehemiah 2:17-20

❓ *Why does he say the broken wall and the fire damage is such a problem (v 17)?*

❓ *What encouragement does Nehemiah give the people as he tells them his proposal?*

❓ *What two responses do his words receive (v 18, 19)?*

❓ *How does Nehemiah reply to his opponents?*

❓ *How is his answer both humble and firm?*

Notice that the hand of the Lord being on his people (v 18) does not create passivity or promote inaction—rather, it causes them to put their own hands to the work! Nehemiah's combination of faith and action is spreading now to the rest of Israel.

The New Testament encourages believers to "always give yourselves fully to the work of the Lord, because you know that your labour in the Lord is not in vain" (1 Corinthians 15:58). Why? Because the resurrection of Jesus means that death has been defeated and that God's people will live in his place for ever. His hand is upon us, and he has given us work to do. Nothing we do for him, for his kingdom, can ever be "in vain".

🔺 Pray

Thank God for the work he has given you to do, in his world and for his people. Ask him to help you do it faithfully and well, with patience and joy—no matter what the opposition.

Bible in a year: 2 Kings 16 – 20

Rebuilding begins

There are two ways to read this section. You can read it as a boring list of names. Or you can hear the hammers pounding, the workers' shouts…

And you can feel the tremendous energy and excitement of a large group of people accomplishing an apparently impossible task together.

Read Nehemiah 3:1, 32

This description of the wall-work begins and ends at the Sheep Gate, in the north-eastern corner of Jerusalem. It moves anti-clockwise, in a big circle.

- *Who are the first builders described (v 1)?*
- *What do they do after building the wall?*
- *What does this suggest about how the Jews think of their work on the wall?*

The wall

Read Nehemiah 3:2-12

- *What is the sour note in verse 5?*
- *How do the Tekoan nobles compare to other high-ranking men (v 9, 12)?*

The excitement of verses 6-12 is in seeing how so many very different people all pitch in together to accomplish this task.

- *Glance back over verses 1-12, and identify some of the various groups of people working together (e.g. by trade, city of origin, family).*

The big point of Nehemiah 3's list of names is: they were (almost) all in it together. Rulers and perfume-makers (v 8-9) presumably didn't get their hands dirty all that often; but they did for this wall. This chapter is a picture of what happens when God's people, humbly and determinedly, work hard together.

Apply

- *How does this passage both encourage and challenge you when it comes to your "hard work" as part of your church?*
- *Where are the areas you are, or can be, serving like a perfume-maker?*
- *When, and why, are you tempted to act like a Tekoan noble?*

The gates

Read Nehemiah 3:13-32

- *What do the descriptions of the gate repairs in verses 13-15 have in common?*
- *Imagine you live in Jerusalem, surrounded by enemies (see 2:19). How would this detail be hugely important to you?*

Read Nehemiah 1:3

- *What difference to the people's feelings and self-perception do you think the achievements of chapter 3 would have made?*

Pray

God is mentioned only once in chapter 3, but we know from 2:20 that he is the one making it all happen. Identify some ways God is working in your life, and praise him for what he is doing.

Bible in a year: Psalm 87 – 89

A people who trust and act

Opposition will come to every follower of Jesus, guaranteed. Before he went to the cross, Jesus himself promised it (John 15:20). The question is, how will we respond?

Ridicule

Read Nehemiah 4:1-6

We've seen (1:3; 2:17) that one goal of Nehemiah's wall-work is to remove the shame of God's people.

- How does 4:1-3 show that this is a continuing issue?

The Jews of Jerusalem might be excused if they choose to respond viciously to their enemies. But they don't.

- What do they do instead (v 4-6)?
- What do they say to their enemies (v 4-5: warning—trick question!)?
- What does their example teach us about how to respond to opposition to the work of the gospel?

Apply

- Are you facing opposition and/or derision for living as a Christian and working hard for God? How?

Trust justice to God. And then get on with working hard. Just as Nehemiah trusted God by praying, and then acted boldly, so God's people did then, and still can today.

---- TIME OUT ----

Read Romans 12:14-21

- How have we seen the people of Jerusalem living out these words?

- How is verse 14 even more radical?

How can we live like this? We have the privilege of the ultimate example: the Lord Jesus. On the cross, his enemies despised and mocked him (Luke 23:35-38). Yet on the cross, Jesus prayed for their forgiveness (v 34) and then died to offer them eternal life. Amazing!

Resolution

Read Nehemiah 4:7-14

- How does the opposition grow?
- How do the Jews again respond with trust and action (v 9, 14)?

Read Nehemiah 4:15-23

- How does Nehemiah interpret the failure of his enemies' plans (v 15)?
- How does he encourage the people in case of an attack (v 20)?

Notice once again that relying on God's strength (v 20) doesn't undermine the vigilance and activity of God's people—it undergirds it (v 21-23).

Pray

Thank God for this wonderful picture of how to respond to opposition. Ask him to help you see what this response would look like in your own circumstances.

Bible in a year: Proverbs 13

Friday 1 August — Nehemiah 5:1-19

Trouble within

Nehemiah 3 – 4 shows us remarkable unity—priests, nobles and common folk all working together to rebuild the wall. But now we discover that all is not well.

People struggling
Read Nehemiah 5:1-5

It appears that some of the people are not happy to be spending their time working on the wall. They're concerned about having enough food to survive (v 2).

- *How do verses 3-4 outline the dire situation of these people?*
- *Who is to blame, do they say (v 1)?*

The leader intervenes
Read Nehemiah 5:6-13

How have the wealthier Jews (the "nobles and officials" of v 7) been wronging their poorer brothers (v 7-8, 10)?

- *How does Nehemiah feel (v 6)?*

It's worth remembering that Nehemiah is a leader, who is not numbered among the people having to sell their land to buy their food. Yet he still identifies with them, and is moved emotionally by this economic injustice.

Apply

- *What we get angry about reveals what we really care about. What makes you most angry? What does this reveal about you?*

The nobles react with silence to the charges (v 8) and Nehemiah then calls for repentance and restitution (v 10-11).

- *How do the nobles' words and actions in verses 12-13 demonstrate that they have truly repented?*

A greater leader
Read Nehemiah 5:14-19

Nehemiah prays again...

- *What does he ask for (v 19)?*
- *According to verses 14-18, what is the "all" that he has "done"?*

Nehemiah was a great leader who was deeply angered at ungodliness and who served God's people at personal cost. He points us towards a far greater leader who also became angry at ungodliness (John 2:13-17) and paid a far greater price in order to bless and serve God's people (see 2 Corinthians 8:9).

This should prompt us to ask: in what ways are we like the struggling "men and their wives" in Nehemiah 5:1, versus the wealthy, thoughtless nobles? And do we react as the latter did—coming to a greater leader, Jesus, in our trials and struggles, and begging for help; and repenting and changing when that greater leader points out where we are taking advantage of others.

Apply

- *Which do you need to do now (maybe both!)?*

Bible in a year: Ezekiel 37 – 42

Intimidation tactics

"Through many dangers, toils, and snares I have already come; Tis grace hath brought me safe thus far, and grace will lead me home," as John Newton's famous hymn says.

Nehemiah's enemies now resort to psychological warfare. Their weapon is fear. But, as we'll see, God's grace is leading Nehemiah through the dangers and snares his enemies are setting in his path.

The first tactic

Read Nehemiah 6:1-9

After failing to ambush and harm Nehemiah (v 1-4), his enemies turn to other tactics.

- ❓ *What emotional response do Nehemiah's enemies want to provoke? How do they attempt to create this response?*
- ❓ *Why do they want him to react this way (v 9)?*
- ❓ *How does Nehemiah in fact respond (v 9)?*

Apply

When we're afraid, we often become less productive in doing the work God has called us to. When faced with fear-producing situations, we need to turn to God, not away from him, and seek his strength and presence.

- ❓ *Why not memorise Isaiah 41:10 for next time you're afraid: "Do not fear, for I am with you; do not be dismayed, for I am your God. I will strengthen you and help you; I will uphold you with my righteous right hand."*

The second tactic

Read Nehemiah 6:10-14

We've already seen an attempt to harm Nehemiah (v 2) and to make him fearful so he'll cease his work (v 9). Now here's another psychological weapon...

- ❓ *What does the ploy seem to be this time?*
- ❓ *How does Nehemiah respond (v 11, 14)?*

Shemaiah is a Jew; but he's a wolf in sheep's clothing. Nehemiah sees right through him, and refuses to quit his work and damage his reputation by acting like a coward.

Read Nehemiah 6:15-19

- ❓ *What is Tobiah still trying to do (v 19)?*
- ❓ *But what happens despite the intimidation (v 15)?*
- ❓ *How do Nehemiah's enemies feel about this, and why (v 16)?*

In verses 9 and 14, it's the presence and protection of God which is the reason Nehemiah isn't afraid! And it's the same thing—God's help—which means that the enemies of God's people are afraid. It is good to be on God's side—and terrifying not to be.

Pray

Thank God that his work gets done despite opposition to his people. Praise God for numbering you among his people, so that you can love his presence, instead of being afraid of it.

Bible in a year: Luke 23 – 24

Grace for daily burdens

This is a psalm of rage, power, pomp and noise. If it were a musical genre, it would be heavy metal. "May God arise!" And when he does, watch out, world—and church.

Read Psalm 68

Big God—big prayers?

David is praying for God to break in, and for his enemies to be blown away into death (v 1-2). He worships a God of limitless power, who invested that power in the redemption of his people from Egypt (v 7-10).

This is our God. He rides on the clouds (v 4, 32-34), he stands at the head of mighty heavenly armies (v 17), and he will conquer every enemy who comes against him (v 21). Hear the chords of this music as they thunder out the praise of Israel's God, and join the worship.

Apply

- What or who do you revert to trusting in when life is hard?
- What crises has God rescued you from? Remember them, and thank him again for his grace.
- Are there problems you've lost heart about, or are you praying often about them?

TIME OUT

Read Exodus 15:11-13

Compare these verses to this psalm. Celebrate the truths they tell you of your God in Christ.

Deliverance, gospel-style

Our mighty God shows the might of his grace too. He summons a throng of women (Psalm 68:11) to proclaim his word. David is probably looking back to Deborah's leadership of Israel (Judges 4 – 5).

We too are called to proclaim the victory of God. We do so as those who should have been "scattered" by him (Psalm 68:14), and yet who by grace find ourselves in Christ and on the winning side. Although we should be led as captives towards judgment, we are led captive by grace, to glory. This is the freedom of the gospel. And it's truly awesome.

- Read verse 18 and Ephesians 4:8. Is God a giving or a taking God? In what sense?

Apply

- Does your answer to the previous question challenge how you naturally think of God in some way? How?

Pray

Now this majestic Saviour leads us in a procession of praise to the Father. He is our powerful, awesome God (Psalm 68:24-27; see Hebrews 2:11-13); the God who gives the strength of his grace to his people (Psalm 68:35). Spend time praising him.

Bible in a year: 1 Thessalonians 4 – 5

Not just a list of names

This chapter begins with a sentence which, back in chapter 1, seemed most unlikely ever to be uttered: "After the wall had been rebuilt and I had set the doors in place…"

Nehemiah has completed the wall! What next?

The leader
Read Nehemiah 7:1-4

Nehemiah chooses two leaders: Hanani and Hananiah.

Pray

We last heard of Hanani way back in 1:2. Briefly recall all that God has done through his leader, Nehemiah, and his people since then. Praise him for doing all these things. Then praise him for what you have noticed him doing in and around you during the last week.

> ❓ What reasons does Nehemiah give for choosing Hananiah as a key leader?

Apply

Churches often choose their leaders on the basis of intelligence, speaking ability or Bible knowledge. These are good things but we'd be wise to remember the words of the 19th-century pastor Robert Murray M'Cheyne: "It is not great talents God blesses, so much as great likeness to Jesus. A holy minister is an awe-ful weapon in the hand of God."

> ❓ What do you value most highly in your church leaders?
>
> ❓ How do you think we can spot true respect for, or "fear of", God?

❓ *How does Nehemiah, ever the man of action, provide for Jerusalem's safety?*

The people
Read Nehemiah 7:5

Nehemiah's desire to enrol the people by genealogy must be a good one, since it's put into his heart by God! We're now going to read a long section, consisting of lots of names of the Jews who first returned to Jerusalem from exile in Babylon.

In Israel, genealogy mattered enormously. It proved your place in God's people and gave you identity. This is one of the reasons why Jesus was so radical when he said his true family wasn't his biological mother, father, and siblings, bur rather those who do the will of God (Mark 3:31-35). So Paul wrote that: "Those who have faith are children of Abraham", i.e. "Israel" (Galatians 3:7).

Don't be bored by these verses. Instead, as you read them, remember that these are your (spiritual) ancestors. This is your family tree!

Scan-read Nehemiah 7:6-73a

Pray

Thank God that through faith you are part of this people. Thank him that the Old Testament is the history of his work in your family tree. Praise him for protecting and providing for your ancestors then, and for you today.

Bible in a year: Leviticus 22 – 24

Tuesday 5 August
Nehemiah 7:73b – 8:12

Tears and laughter

Most of us have had an experience in our lives that left us not knowing whether to laugh or cry. Our flood of emotion could have gone either way—perhaps both at the same time!

Here, we find a whole city of people crying and laughing.

The words of the Lord
Read Nehemiah 7:73b – 8:8

The wall has been completed for only a few days—compare 6:15 and 8:2.

- What do the people ask for (v 1)?

Ezra, like Nehemiah, had held a prestigious position in the Persian court. He had returned to Jerusalem some years before Nehemiah (see the book of Ezra). But whereas Nehemiah's mission was to rebuild God's city for God's people to live in, Ezra's was to teach God's people how to live God's way—to re-establish loving obedience of God's law.

- What do verses 1-8 tell us about the people's attitude to God's law?

Apply

- How similar, or different, is your attitude when you hear God's word read aloud or read it yourself?
- We probably don't bow with our faces to the ground (v 6)—but how do you revere and worship the Lord, whose word you're hearing?

The joy of the Lord
Read Nehemiah 8:9-12

- How did the people respond as they heard how God told them to live (end of v 9)?
- Why did they react like this, do you think?
- What are they told to do instead (v 10, 12)?

Grieving and weeping is the right response to hearing God's law, because as we hear of God's perfect standards, we see how far short we fall of the people we should be, and need to be. But grief is not the only emotion God's word should inspire, because in it, God shows us that he has done what we cannot do: made a way for us to become perfect in his sight. The Old Testament law outlined the sacrificial system, which kept sinners in relationship with God; and the New Testament tells of the ultimate sacrifice, the one who makes us perfect in God's sight. God is strong enough to do what we are too weak to do ourselves; so we do not only grieve, we know great joy too. We cry, and then we laugh.

Pray

Spend time confessing to God how you have broken his perfect laws recently. (Perhaps use the Ten Commandments in Exodus 20:1-17 as a prompt.) Grieve over your sinfulness. Perhaps even weep.

Then spend time thanking God that, through Jesus' life and death, you are perfect, sinless, in his sight. Know the joy of forgiveness!

Bible in a year: 2 Kings 21 – 25

The joy of obedience

We've seen God's people's grief and joy as they hear and understand God's word. Now we see Jerusalem's residents move from hearing and understanding to obeying.

Reading God's law
Read Nehemiah 8:13

❷ *Who is sitting down with the priests and Levites (i.e. the experts) to study God's law?*

What a wonderful thing! These were the men who would set the spiritual tone in each home in Jerusalem. It was their example that would be followed.

▼ Apply

❷ *Are you the head of a family? What example do you set your household when it comes to God's word? Have you recognised and accepted your responsibility to your family?*

❷ *Are you a member of a family? Do you pray for your husband or father, that he would lead your household well? Do you let him lead you into joyful obedience of God's word?*

A new discovery
Read Nehemiah 8:14-15

❷ *What do these men discover that God has commanded them to do (v 14)?*

···· TIME OUT ····························

To learn more about the Feast of Tabernacles, **read Leviticus 23:33-44 and Deuteronomy 16:13-15.**

❷ *What is the point of this tent-dwelling festival (Leviticus 23:42-43)?*

In a similar way, God gives his people today the Lord's Supper and baptism, as "living history exhibits"—ways of remembering and picturing how he has saved us through the Lord Jesus.

Obeying God's law
Read Nehemiah 8:16-17

❷ *What do the people do in response to this discovery in God's word?*

The massive popular participation ("the whole company") and the fact that the booths are everywhere is particularly impressive because this feast hasn't been kept properly for centuries (v 17).

❷ *How do the people respond (end of v 17)?*

❷ *What does this show us about obeying God's word as part of God's people?*

Read Nehemiah 8:18

❷ *How does this verse emphasise the continuing obedience of the people?*

▲ Pray

God does not give us commands to burden or bore us but for our joy! Pray that you would not simply obey God this week but that you would know joy as you do so.

Bible in a year: Psalm 90 – 92

A prayer to God, part 1

Feasting now gives way to fasting and confession. But surprisingly, the fasting and confession begin to mingle freely with soaring praise. What's going on here?!

Confession and praise

Read Nehemiah 9:1-5

These verses show us what a healthy practice of confessing our sins to God looks like. The reading of God's perfect law should lead to imperfect people confessing their sins (v 3). It should lead to imperfect people praising God for his uncompromising perfection (v 5).

Apply

Bible-centred churches will be churches who give regular opportunities for confessing sin as the people of God.

- *How does this happen in your church? And during it, how much do you focus on your sin, and on your need to confess? Do you pray with your heart, as well as with your lips?*

Praise the Lord

The Levites urge the people to praise God (v 5), and now we're swept into a magnificent prayer—one of the greatest of the Old Testament. This prayer gives us a panoramic view of God's work from creation and throughout his dealings with Israel, his people.

Read Nehemiah 9:5-15

- *What is the people's first reason for praising God (v 6)?*
- *What is their second reason for praising God (v 7-8)? What does this part of Old Testament history tell us about God's character?*
- *What is their third reason for praising God (v 9-15)?*

Notice the verses that surround those which talk about God's commands (v 13-14). They're all about what God did—how God saw, sent, knew, led, gave. God's laws are not given so that people know how to become his people, but so that those who have become his people know how to live as his people.

Pray

Think of a couple (or more) of amazing things God did in Bible times. Then choose a couple of amazing things he has done in the history of your country and a couple from your own life. Praise him for them!

Read Nehemiah 9:16-25

- *What did Israel do in the past (v 16-18)?*
- *What is amazing about God's response (v 17, 19-25)? What does this tell us about him?*

Pray

Use verse 17b to praise God for who he is!

Bible in a year: Proverbs 14 – 15

A prayer to God, part 2

In this wonderful prayer, God's people had reached the promised land, full of "all kinds of good things" (v 25). Now it is recalled what life was like for them there.

A cycle of sin
Read Nehemiah 9:25-31

- How did Israel respond to God's goodness (v 25-26)?
- How did God respond to Israel's actions (v 27a)?
- How did Israel continue to experience God's undeserved compassion (v 27)?

Verses 26-31 are repetitive! There's a cycle of sin, warning, suffering, repentance and deliverance. It's the people's repeated sinfulness that begins the cycle again; and it's God's ongoing compassion that means Israel goes on being rescued from the consequences of their disobedience.

It's depressing to see what God's people are like: disobedient, rebellious, blasphemous, evildoers, arrogant, stubborn and stiffnecked (i.e. refusing to bow to God as ruler).

And it's wonderful to see what God himself is like: compassionate, rescuing, patient, merciful and gracious.

Life after exile
Read Nehemiah 9:32-37

The prayer now reaches the present day: the time of Nehemiah and his contemporaries. They acknowledge that the exile was just (v 33). But, as we've seen, now they have returned from exile; they have rebuilt Jerusalem and placed themselves under God's law once more, to live in his place as his people.

- So in light of this, what is so surprising about what they say in verse 36?
- Why do the returned Jews say this (v 37)?
- How is life in the land for these people different to how it was when God first gave it to their ancestors?

Apply

I find it easy to be amazed by, and a little smug about, Israel's folly in always circling back to the same sins. But then I think of the sins I keep on committing, over and over again...

- Are there ways in which you repeatedly disobey God, even despite your best intentions?
- How does admitting the circularity of your sin help you to appreciate God's forgiveness?

Spend some time now thanking God for the cross of Jesus, which has secured full and final forgiveness, and abundant and undeserved blessing, for you.

Bible in a year: Ezekiel 43 – 48

Commitment

True prayer always changes the one who prays. Israel has prayed. Now we see them change.

In view of our prayer

Read Nehemiah 9:38

❓ *What step are the leaders of Israel taking?*

❓ *What indicates the seriousness of this step?*

Read Nehemiah 10:1-27

Notice Nehemiah's name is listed first—great leadership!

❓ *Why do you think the writer goes to the trouble of listing all the individual names of those who signed this sealed document?*

A curse and an oath

Read Nehemiah 10:28-29

❓ *So far, the chapter has focused on the leaders. What is being emphasised here?*

❓ *What solemn commitment do they make (v 29)?*

❓ *What is so radical about this commitment (especially bearing in mind 9:16-17, 26, 29, 34)?*

This is the oath—but this is not only an oath, it also contains "a curse".

❓ *If they disobey, what do they accept will be the consequences (10:29)?*

TIME OUT

Though the word isn't used here, this is a covenant. And throughout the Old Testament, entering into a covenant with God is a serious thing, because part of making a covenant is accepting that curses will result from breaking it. **Read Deuteronomy 27:11-26** to see an example.

This is, of course, bad news for sinners, who can never keep the covenant perfectly. **Read Galatians 3:13-14** and praise Jesus for taking the curse in order to bring us the blessings reserved for covenant-keepers!

Read Nehemiah 10:30-39

❓ *Which specific commands are now highlighted?*

❓ *How might the people feel the cost and inconvenience, day by day, of what they're committing to?*

Apply

The call of the New Testament is not to live God's way so that we can be blessed as covenant-keepers, but to live his way because we are already blessed, through Christ, as covenant-keepers.

❓ *When are you most tempted to cut corners when it comes to obeying God? How will you change?*

❓ *When do you most need to remember that it's Christ's covenant-keeping, not yours, that secures your blessing?*

Bible in a year: John 1 – 2

God in the depths

In one of the darkest of psalms we discover the brightest hope.

Overwhelming

Read Psalm 69

Overwhelmed, abandoned and opposed…

❓ *Has this ever been you? What did you do? And what did God do?*

There is a man in the Bible who was opposed by sinners, abandoned by God and overwhelmed by our sin and its punishment. He tells us that the whole Bible is all about him, and that includes this psalm.

❓ *Read Luke 24:26-27. Then reread Psalm 69:13-29. Who are you looking at? How does this change the way you read the psalm?*

Psalm 69 traces David's terrifying experience of suffering. One of the images is of facing a storm with its floodwaters. In Jesus, we meet the God who not only rules the storms but who has endured the most violent storm of all. When Jesus went to the cross, he knew the storm of God's wrath breaking over him. Our sins were the depths he was plunged into, and God's wrath against our sin was the engulfing flood which he endured.

The New Testament cites or refers to this psalm over a dozen times, always linking it with the life of Jesus Christ, especially in his sufferings. It is *his* psalm. Above all, the sufferings he experienced, which the psalm prefigures, are the sufferings due to us for our sins—our punishment, which Jesus endured. He took the storm, and took it for us.

Safe

Even with life's currents and deluges, we are absolutely sure of our safe arrival in heaven. Jesus has endured God's wrath, and taken it in our place. We receive our forgiveness through faith alone, and God's Spirit assures us that, come what may, we are united to Christ for all of life and eternity. We are safe. Whatever we face in this life, as the hymn says, "The wind and waves still know his voice".

The great Reformer John Calvin wrote of this wonderful psalm:

"Let us learn, while God spares us, to meditate on this truth, and to take the help which it is designed to give us under suffering, that even in the deepest depths of adversity, faith may hold us up, and what is more, may lift us up to God. There is, as Paul testifies (Romans 8:39), no height nor depth which can separate us from the infinite love of him who swallows up all depths, yes, even hell itself."

Pray

❓ *How do you need to let this psalm encourage you today?*

❓ *How does it move you to pour out praise and gratitude to Jesus?*

Do so now.

Bible in a year: 2 Thessalonians 1 – 3

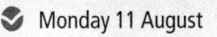

Moving to Jerusalem

The wall has been rebuilt, the city of Jerusalem protected… but will anyone actually live in it?!

Present moving
Read Nehemiah 11:1-36

- *What indication is there in verses 1-2 that perhaps not everyone **wanted** to live in Jerusalem?*
- *What glimpses into temple worship do we catch here (v 15-18, 22-23)?*

This is another long list of names! But notice what mattered to those who were moving into God's city or lived outside it in God's land. Their community was ordered, with men in charge of the city's districts (e.g. v 9) and jobs allocated to the residents (e.g. v 19). And some of them had the great privilege of living where their ancestors had done, before the exile (v 20).

Past return
Read Nehemiah 12:1-26

This list looks back in time, listing the people who returned to Jerusalem between 538 BC, when the first exiles came home from Babylon, and Nehemiah's day.

TIME OUT
Read Haggai 1:12-15

- *What motivated this first generation of returnees to come back to Jerusalem?*

Nehemiah 11 records the work of God that took place in Nehemiah's time, and under his leadership. As we've seen, walls rose from rubble and a whole people committed themselves to loving and serving God.

But Nehemiah 12 reminds us that much had gone before. What God did through Nehemiah was a continuation of what he had been doing through many years before. And so today, we should pray for and work for and hope for great works of God in our churches and our lives. But we should also remember and praise God for all he has done before our day—particularly when our "achievements" are built on what he did through our spiritual parents and grandparents.

Pray

Praise God now. Praise him for some things he is doing in your church and in your life. Praise him for things he has done in your church or family or community before your own time. Praise him for what he did through his Son 2,000 years before our day, upon which everything he is doing today, and will do in the future, is built.

Bible in a year: Leviticus 25 – 27

Singing for joy

Real joy wants to express itself. Have you ever been so happy that you just had to shout or dance or burst into song?

We don't really understand this passage until we hear the sounds it describes. So let's listen as we read.

The party
Read Nehemiah 12:27-43

Nehemiah is a man who gets things done, and he knows how to throw a party! He's the event planner for these celebrations (12:31).

- List all the sounds this passage describes. Which instruments are used? Who is singing? What other sounds are there?
- Who is ultimately responsible for what the people are feeling (v 43)?
- Who can hear (v 43)?

Verses 27-30 describe the significant logistical effort invested in pulling together this musical extravaganza. And it's Levites, professional musicians, who are playing. For Nehemiah, it's clear that an exuberant display of joy is helped, not hindered, by careful preparation and skilful musical performance.

Apply

We're seeing God's people gather together to praise him.

- So what principles do we learn here about our own gatherings as God's people on Sundays?
- Apart from making music, what else do the Levites and priests do (v 30, 43)?

The money
Read Nehemiah 12:44-47

- What do the people do (v 44, 47)? Why (v 44-45)?

Notice the mention of the time of David and Solomon in verses 45-46. These were Israel's greatest kings; their reigns were the highpoint of Israel's history.

- How does their mention cast Nehemiah and his efforts in a favourable light?

TIME OUT

Read Ephesians 5:18-21

- How do these verses help us to understand what is happening in Nehemiah 12, and what should be happening in our churches?

Apply

All too often, we live as Christians, but we don't have very much (or any) joy about it. How can we experience the same depth of joy as the people did in Nehemiah's day?

- Dwell on what God has done for you: his saving of you; his work in you; his gifts to you; his presence with you. These truths will prompt joy!

Pray

Ask God to give your church a more and more joyful time as you gather each week.

Bible in a year: 1 Chronicles 1 – 4

Wednesday 13 August — Nehemiah 13:1-14

It was found written

Chapter 12 reads as though it could end the book. But Nehemiah's not finished yet. The wall has been rebuilt and dedicated; but there are still more reforms to be enacted.

Excluded

Read Nehemiah 13:1-3

Do these verses, with their approving description of Israel separating from all those of foreign descent, justify racism? Let's look closer.

- Why did the people separate themselves from those of foreign descent (v 1-2)?

···· TIME OUT ····

Read the passage that Nehemiah and company read: **Deuteronomy 23:3-6**. If you have time, read the story of Israel, Moab and Balaam in **Numbers 22 – 24**.

Racism is not motivating the people's actions, but rather a desire to obey God and not be misled and pulled away from a commitment to God by foreigners who do not worship the one true God. This isn't really about being "Israelite" or "foreign" but being a worshipper of God or a rebel against him.

■ Apply

These verses are not anti-immigration!

- But what challenging applications should God's people draw from them today, do you think?

Threw out

Read Nehemiah 13:4-9

- Who does Eliashib the priest give a room to within the temple building?
- What's so terrible about this? (Hint: look back to 2:10 and 4:7-8.)
- Why is Eliashib able to do this (13:6)?
- How does Nehemiah respond when he finds out (v 7-9)?

Rebuked

Read Nehemiah 13:10-14

- Why had the Levites and singers left the temple (v 10)?
- How does Nehemiah respond (v 12-14)?

Things are the opposite of how they should be. Instead of God's ministers keeping the contributions of God's people in this room, God's enemy has been storing his personal wealth there! And Nehemiah won't stand for God's temple being misused. In this, he is a forerunner of God's ultimate chosen leader, a man who would also grow angry when he entered the temple to find people using it for their own selfish ends (Mark 11:15-17).

■ Apply

Nehemiah and Jesus were both passionate about God's standards and God's people.

- Are you? How does this show itself?

Bible in a year: Psalm 93 – 95

The Sabbath issue

We've seen that Nehemiah is a man of prayer and a man of action, focused on serving God and skilled in practical matters. Here, his character stands out with particular clarity.

Warning of wrath
Read Nehemiah 13:15-18

"Remember the Sabbath day by keeping it holy. Six days you shall labour and do all your work, but the seventh day is a sabbath to the Lord your God. On it you shall not do any work…" (Exodus 20:8-10). That's the fifth commandment.

- Why is what Nehemiah sees so serious?
- How does he describe what's happening (Nehemiah 13:17)?
- Quite apart from the fifth commandment, why else should the Jews avoid working on the Sabbath and so disobeying God (v 18)?

Nehemiah is able to "think vertically"—he looks at any given situation and his first thought is what God says about it.

Apply

- How often do you consciously think about what God thinks of something that you, or others, are doing?
- Is there anything you're doing which you know, deep down, God says is wrong? Will you stop?

Having spoken theological truth to the Jewish nobles, Nehemiah now takes practical measures. Let's see what he does.

Shutting the doors
Read Nehemiah 13:19-22

- What four things does Nehemiah do to make sure Sabbath rest will not be ignored in Jerusalem?

The Sabbath—Saturday—is deeply precious to Nehemiah. As Christians, we now gather to worship on Sunday (see Acts 20:7; 1 Corinthians 16:2). But we might ask: does God want us to cease all work on Sundays, just as the Jews did (or were supposed to) on the Sabbath? And what would that "work" be?

TIME OUT
Read Hebrews 4:1-10

- When did God rest (v 3b-4)?

The ultimate "rest" is found in enjoying life with God in his perfect creation.

- God still offers this kind of rest (v 1). How do people fail to enter it—and how can we therefore enjoy it (v 2)?

This is not an experience that any amount of work can win us (v 10); it is God who brings us into his perfect, eternal rest, through faith in Jesus. We enjoy rest each day, as we joyfully love and obey Christ; we will enjoy ultimate rest every day eternally, as we live with him. And whenever we rest from our labours now, we can remember that ultimately, our work cannot save us; and that wonderfully, it doesn't need to. Praise God for true rest in Christ.

Bible in a year: Proverbs 16

Relationship issues

Is there anything you believe in so strongly that you're willing to risk offending people in order to stand up for your convictions?

The wrong wives
Read Nehemiah 13:23-27

- What does Nehemiah see and hear in verses 23-24?
- What do you make of his response (v 25)?

This may seem like an overreaction…

- But what reasons does he give for being this firm in verse 26 and verse 27?

TIME OUT

Read 1 Kings 11:1-8

1 Kings 11:2 repeats a divine command and warning found already in Exodus 34:11-16.

Nehemiah is passionate about the purity of God's people—not racial purity but spiritual purity. This passion is a godly one, extending all the way back to God's command at Mount Sinai. And his logic is sound: if even wise Solomon couldn't withstand the God-dishonouring influence of wives who worshipped false gods, how will normal Israelites possibly do so?

The wrong father-in-law
Read Nehemiah 13:28-31a

Nehemiah's still not finished with his reforms.

- What does he do (v 28, 31)? Why (v 29-30)?

The thing that unites all Nehemiah's actions is his passion for God's people to worship God properly. He wants their houses, and the temple, to be places where God is known, honoured, obeyed and enjoyed. That is, after all, why he's been so eager throughout this book to lead God's people back to Jerusalem.

If Nehemiah's actions seem extreme, could it be because our passion for knowing and serving God has grown cold? He was willing to risk his reputation, content to offend people, to do all he could to preserve and promote true worship.

Apply

- How passionate are you about worshipping God properly? How passionate are you about encouraging and challenging other believers to do so?
- When are you most likely to avoid risking offence, rather than boldly insisting that God is obeyed?

Pray

"Do not be yoked … with unbelievers" (2 Corinthians 6:14). Ask God for wisdom to know how to be a good friend to those who don't know Jesus, so you can point them to him. But ask God, too, to help you make sure you don't end up being influenced by the conduct of friends who don't want to obey him.

Bible in a year: Daniel 1 – 6

Remember me

This great man of prayer closes his book with a heartfelt cry to God.

Read Nehemiah 13:31b

- How exactly does Nehemiah address God here?
- What is the significance of this? How have we seen this view of God shaping Nehemiah's life and actions throughout the book?

In Nehemiah 4:14, Nehemiah urged the Jews to "remember the Lord". That's not a surprising thing to do—people are very quick to forget all about God. But here, as in 1:8 and 6:14, he asks God to do the remembering. And here, it is himself who he wants God to remember. But God doesn't forget about people—they don't somehow slip his mind. What's going on?!

By asking God to remember him "with favour", Nehemiah is committing himself to God's judgment and placing himself in God's hands. He's not asking God not to forget him—he's asking God, when he thinks of him, to do so favourably, and therefore to act towards him with favour.

- Think back through the book. Who has Nehemiah annoyed, offended or upset?
- What does 13:31b reveal to have been Nehemiah's priority all along?

TIME OUT

Nehemiah isn't the only biblical character to pursue God's good opinion of him rather than the good opinion of other people.

Read 1 Corinthians 4:1-4

- What is Paul's attitude about who judges him? Whose good opinion does he seek? Why?
- Why is it liberating to live with this perspective on life?

▼ Apply

- Does your desire for the good opinion of others ever hinder your walk with Christ? How?
- What are the areas of life where you care too much about being popular with, or respected by, others?

▲ Pray

Nehemiah was the godly leader of Jerusalem—but he still needed God to "remember him". Centuries later, an ungodly criminal, hanging on a cross, also knew he needed God to "remember me" (Luke 23:42). And the God who hung beside him on his own cross answered with stunning certainty and beauty: "Today you will be with me in paradise" (v 43).

Thank the Lord Jesus that, because of his death and resurrection, you can know that God looks on you with favour.

- When will you need to remember this next week, so that you live boldly for him?

Bible in a year: John 3 – 4

When all else fails

Despair is not an unchristian feeling—but the Christian does heed the clear gospel answer to despair.

Read Psalm 70

Always in need

David is struggling with enemies who would happily see him dead (v 2-3). He is desperate and desperately needy (v 5).

- *What does he do about that, in this psalm (v 1, 5)?*

Danger does not mean that God is absent, and enemies don't mean that God is unloving. He is always with us, always good, always powerful and always ready and able to help.

Apply

- *Do you find it hard to be honest with God, especially when life is really hard? Why / why not?*
- *Do you try to solve all your problems and only come to God when all else fails?*

Always in grace

It is because of all that Jesus endured for us that we can have such confidence in God, even in hard times. How often we collapse into angry self-pity or prayerless desolation, when things go wrong. We fume that God hasn't given us what we feel we deserve, and we fear that we were never safe in his love in the first place.

Remember that when we feel lonely and afraid, we have one who suffered in our place. As we saw in Psalm 69, these psalms which explore our anguish actually show us our Saviour, who took it all at the cross for us.

Read the psalm again, as if it were coming from Jesus' heart.

Because he was cut off in his sufferings, all who trust in him are eternally loved and safe. Believe it! And remember, too, that Jesus is Immanuel—God with us. Because of the gift of his indwelling Spirit, he has never gone—and will never go—away.

Apply

- *Which is more important—feeling that we are safe or actually being safe because of God's committed love in Christ?*
- *When do you most need to remember the answer to the previous question?*
- *God is glorified in our dependence on him. What problems will you bring to him today?*
- *What situations are you tempted to feel despair in? Why do you think that is, and what truths from this psalm can help you to fight those feelings?*

Pray

Read Hebrews 13:5-6 and John 14:23 and use them to fuel your prayers today.

Bible in a year: 1 Timothy 1 – 3

ACTS: Do not be silent

As we rejoin Acts, Paul is on his missionary journey around Greece. Athens is behind him and he is heading west, to Corinth—where he'll spend the next 18 months.

New friends

Read Acts 18:1-6

Pontus, Aquila and Priscilla's home region was in modern-day Turkey.

Read Acts 2:1-12

- How might the message of Jesus have reached Pontus (see v 9)?
- How did Paul support himself when he first arrived in Corinth (18:3)?
- What allowed him to "[devote] himself exclusively to preaching" (v 5)?

Silas and Timothy brought news, and a few concerns, from the believers in Thessalonica (v 5). In response Paul wrote the letters we call 1 and 2 Thessalonians.

A second vision

For the second time God gives Paul a vision (see Acts 18:9). This time, however, the Lord himself speaks.

Read Acts 18:7-11

- What happened before Paul received the vision (v 8)?
- But what do Jesus' words in verse 9 suggest about how Paul was feeling?
- Given Paul's journeys so far, what might have tempted him to fearfulness?
- What tools did the Lord give Paul to defuse his fear (v 10)?

Apply

- Are there past experiences that you are fearful will repeat themselves? Do these fears discourage you from living and speaking for him with confidence?
- How does the Lord's promise, "I am with you," speak to those fears?

A first trial

We've seen Paul beaten, stoned, and left for dead. This is the first (though not the last) time we see him before a judge.

Read Acts 18:12-17

- What charge was brought against Paul (v 13)?
- Why did Gallio dismiss it (v 15)?

So Paul was free to remain in Corinth, proclaiming Christ. And the promise of verse 10 came true—there was in due course a church in the city, to which he could write the two letters that bear its name.

Apply

- Think of an area of life where you are finding it hard to live all-out for Jesus. Can you think of a promise he has made that, if you live as though it's true (and it is!), would change your perspective and your actions?

Bible in a year: Numbers 1 – 4

A quick turnaround

Here are eleven verses containing lots of action! Luke closes Paul's second journey, begins his third and introduces us to an important character.

Ending a journey
Read Acts 18:18-23

Luke's mention of a vow (v 18) stokes our curiosity. But don't miss this: these seemingly small details substantiate Luke's reporting. His stories are not myths or legends but historically verifiable accounts. The Christian faith rests on historical realities.

▼ Apply

Behind every believer in Jesus are people who supported them on their way, like the churches of Jerusalem and Antioch did for Paul (v 22).

❓ *Who has held that role for you? How might you report back to them this week about what God is doing in your life?*

Beginning the next

With little fanfare Paul hits the road again. Thus begins his third journey.

❓ *What happened in the cities of Galatia on each journey?*
- 1st journey—Iconium (14:1-3)
- Lystra (14:8-10, 20)
- Derbe (14:21)
- 1st journey, return trip (14:21-22)
- 2nd journey (16:1-4)
- 3rd journey (18:23)

Meanwhile, in Ephesus
Read Acts 18:24-26

❓ *Where was Apollos from (v 24)?*
❓ *How would you describe his giftedness (v 24-26)?*
❓ *How would you describe his personality (v 25-26, 28)?*

John the Baptist prepared the way for Jesus' earthly ministry (Luke 3:15-18). John's disciples shared the good news that the Messiah was coming—news that reached Apollos in Egypt. Yet he hadn't heard the end of the story—that Jesus the Messiah had indeed come, and had died and risen to life. This was the news that Aquila and Priscilla eagerly shared with Apollos.

On to Corinth
Read Acts 18:27-28

❓ *Whose idea was it for Apollos to go to Corinth (v 27)? Who confirmed this plan? How?*
❓ *How did he strengthen the church of Corinth (v 27-28)?*

▼ Apply

❓ *What does verse 27 tell us about how to make significant decisions wisely?*
❓ *In what way do you need to hear this for yourself, or advise it to someone else?*

Bible in a year: 1 Chronicles 5 – 9

Acts 19:1-10 — Wednesday 20 August

In Ephesus

Think of Ephesus as an ancient version of New York City: a key port city with a cosmopolitan vibe, full of expats from around the world.

Ephesus was a hugely significant place: only Rome surpassed it in culture, commerce—and idolatry. How could the gospel thrive, and believers survive, in a place like that?

Getting up to speed

Paul began his third missionary journey in Galatia (18:23), then fulfilled his promise to return to Ephesus, where he had left Aquila and Priscilla (18:19-20).

Read Acts 19:1-3

This is an odd story, but it underscores the challenge of sharing Jesus with the world. Consider the very different types of spiritual conditions the early disciples encountered:

- Jews who studied the Scriptures diligently (17:11)
- Jews who did not (17:1-3, 11)
- Religiously-mixed Samaritans (8:5-8)
- Gentile converts to Judaism (8:27)
- Pagan philosophers (17:18)
- Disciples of John the Baptist (18:25)

John's disciples were pointed in the right direction *(the Messiah is coming)* but hadn't heard the rest of the story.

Read Acts 19:4-7

- ❷ *How did Paul differentiate between John's baptism and Christian baptism (v 4)?*
- ❷ *What did John's disciples do (v 5)?*

Throughout Acts, Luke has reported five marks of conversion—repentance, faith, calling on the Lord, the gift of the Holy Spirit and water baptism.

- ❷ *Which are present here (v 4-6)? What other marks does Luke add?*

Ministering in Ephesus

Read Acts 19:8-10

- ❷ *Where did Paul begin his ministry (v 8)?*
- ❷ *What was his message (v 8)?*
- ❷ *How did some people respond to his message (v 9)?*
- ❷ *What did Paul do next (v 9)?*
- ❷ *How long did he ultimately minister in Ephesus (see 20:31)?*

▼ Apply

- ❷ *Your discussions about the Christian life may not be daily—but how can you ensure they are not only weekly, on Sundays?*

Think about the variety of spiritual conditions and views among those who live or work near you.

- ❷ *How can you explain "the kingdom of God" to each in a way that will be faithful but connect with their particular outlook, hopes and fears?*

Bible in a year: Psalm 96 – 98

Use power carefully

We've seen that Paul addressed the synagogue on the subject of the kingdom of God for three months (v 8). Today's passage shows us the power of that kingdom!

Extraordinary miracles

Read Acts 19:11-12

❷ *What do the effects of Paul's healing ministry (v 12) show about the nature of God's kingdom?*

❷ *Read Isaiah 53:4 and its fulfilment in Matthew 8:16-17. What do the effects of Paul's healing ministry show about Jesus?*

The point of this kind of event is to be a witness to the power of the living Jesus, and to give a glimpse of the perfection of his kingdom. But this was easy to misunderstand—and some thought they'd found a new magic word which would give them greater powers...

Read Acts 19:13-16

❷ *What did these would-be exorcists think the new magic word was (v 13)?*

❷ *What happened to them (v 15-16)?*

The Holy Spirit is like the wind—ever present, ever powerful, ever mysterious (John 3:8). We must not trifle with him; he is the Lord Almighty. And yet he dwells with us, empowering us for acts of service.

🔺 Pray

Thank him for his presence with you and his power in you. Pray that he would be at work through you, in whatever way he chooses, to bring praise and glory to the Lord Jesus.

High honour

Read Acts 19:17-20

❷ *What impact did the story of the would-be exorcists have on the people of Ephesus (v 17-18)?*

🔺 Pray

It is easy to get comfortable with the idols of our hearts and hardened to what the Lord is doing. And sometimes the Lord uses unusual displays of his power to shake our hold on what we love more than him. Ask him to search your heart for things you are putting above him in your life, and ask for grace to give up that idol so that you may experience healing and restoration by his Spirit.

The next plan

Read Acts 19:21-22

❷ *Where does Paul decide to go (v 21)? Where else does he want to visit?*

This sets the plan for the rest of the book. We'll see Paul go to Jerusalem, with seismic results. And we'll see him make his way to Rome, in an unexpected way. And once he reaches that destination, we'll be at the end of the book!

Bible in a year: Proverbs 17 – 18

God works in the silence

Today's passage reminds me of the book of Esther: in both, the author makes no explicit reference to God. But make no mistake—he is there, and he's at work!

Danger

Read Acts 19:23-27

❷ *What was Demetrius' main concern (v 25, 27)?*

TIME OUT

Money and career are powerful idols.

❷ *How might Demetrius' opposition to the gospel message look in your particular context today?*

Read Acts 19:28-31

❷ *How did the crowd feel about Paul's message and why?*

Pray

One way to identify the idols of your heart is to ask, "What makes me angry?" As you answer this question, go a little deeper: what do I want that I am not getting?

Ask the Spirit to reveal what you might not immediately see, and to help you let go of things you love more than Jesus.

Confusion

The Great Theatre of Ephesus still stands, a magnificent open-air stage. Search online for a picture to make this scene more vivid.

❷ *Which believers did the crowd bring into the theatre (v 29)?*

❷ *Who wanted to go but was prevented (v 30-31)?*

Read Acts 19:32-34

Alexander was a Jewish man who presumably wanted to dissociate the Jews from followers of "the Way" (v 23), to show that they posed no threat to the Ephesian goddess Artemis. He never got the chance.

Dismissal

Read Acts 19:35-41

❷ *Who ultimately put an end to the uproar, and why? (There are at least four reasons.)*

In those days city clerks functioned like mayors: they led the local council and reported to the Roman authorities. There is no evidence that he was a believer, but it's evident that some officials know about the faith (v 31).

This dramatic scene may be in view in 2 Corinthians 1:8-11, which Paul penned shortly after leaving Ephesus.

❷ *How have we seen God working "behind the scenes" in this passage?*

Pray

God is always at work, even when he seems silent. Give him thanks for his constant work in your life. Pray that he would sustain you when he seems absent, and that his Spirit would instil courage to follow him.

Bible in a year: Daniel 7 – 12

Encouraging & resurrecting

Macedonia was the first European region to which Paul brought the gospel (Acts 16:12). Now he's heading back there.

Three months in Europe

Read Acts 20:1-6

Paul wrote 2 Corinthians while in Macedonia.

❷ *Read 2 Corinthians 2:12-13. Where did he stop before heading to Macedonia? Why didn't he stay?*

His stay in Greece included time in Corinth. While there he wrote his letter to the Romans.

Notice the transition back to "us" in Acts 20:5. Luke had joined the group on its first trip to Philippi (16:10), but apparently stayed in Philippi after Paul left (17:1). With Paul's return to Macedonia, Luke rejoined the team.

❷ *What did Paul do for the disciples in Ephesus (20:1)? Macedonia (v 2)?*

Apply

To "encourage" is to instil someone with courage or cheer. Think about those you know in your church.

❷ *Who among them is lacking courage or cheer? What word of Jesus-focused encouragement could you give them today?*

Why not text/email/call them right now?!

Seven days in Troas

After three fruitful months Paul's team headed back to Asia Minor, to the city of Troas.

Read Acts 20:7-12

❷ *For what purpose had the disciples gathered (v 7)?*

Today we often refer to church meetings by saying we are "gathering to worship" or "going to church".

❷ *What would be different if instead we said we are "gathering to break bread"? What does that expression emphasise that the ones we tend to use do not?*

The story of Eutychus is a humorous one (though presumably it wasn't at the time!). But don't miss the miracle.

❷ *What did Paul do for Eutychus (v 10)?*

❷ *What effect did his action have on the community of believers (v 12)?*

Pray

Every resurrection reflects the resurrection that stands at the centre of history, the raising of our Lord Jesus from the dead. Eutychus would die someday. But our Lord lives, never to die again! Give thanks for your risen King, who has conquered sin and death for you.

Bible in a year: John 5 – 6

Hope for years to come

In a world which focuses on the short term and that exalts youth, can we really trust that God is a God of the long term, who loves us in old age? Psalm 71 helps us.

Read Psalm 71

- ❓ What experiences of God does the writer look back on (v 5-8, 17)?
- ❓ What is he asking for (v 3-4, 9-13, 18)?

Faithful God

Rock, refuge, fortress and deliverer (v 1-4). Well, God either is all these things or he is none of them. Will we take him at his word? When hard times come—persecution, pain or old age—we really need to fix our hearts on these truths, and on this God (v 5-9). He can be trusted!

The writer of this psalm has known God from his earliest years (v 5-6, 17). He has experienced so much of God's goodness. Now he looks ahead to old age and is fearful; might God discard him then (v 9, 18)? He longs to be able to testify to God's goodness in later life, and needs to be sure that God will be with him when he is old.

▼ Apply

- ❓ How long have you known God's saving love in Jesus?
- ❓ What in your life (apart from the gospel's grace) is fixed and totally reliable? Does your answer surprise you or scare you?
- ❓ What does knowing the gospel do for your heart, day by day (compare v 8)?

Faithful God?

Can the writer really be confident—and, if so, on what grounds? He celebrates God's towering righteousness (v 19). And that is his confidence and ours. God is righteous. He always does what is right. It would be impossible for him ever to fail any of the children of his covenant. Failure to love them would be failure to be righteous, to be the promise-keeping and never-failing God. So yes, we really can be secure. A righteous God must and always will be a faithful God (v 22). And so he will be, right to the last breath of our lives.

▼ Apply

Reread Psalm 71:22-24

- ❓ What does a trusting disciple do? How will these verses change the way you live today?

▲ Pray

Think of three elderly Christians you know. Pray that their hearts would know the assurance of God's love for them, which this psalm speaks of.

- ❓ And why not give them a visit or a phone call this week?

Bible in a year: 1 Timothy 4 – 6

Paul and the elders, part 1

Winston Churchill's "Never give up", Martin Luther King Jr.'s "I have a dream". Some speeches inspire generations. Paul's address to the Ephesian elders is another.

Let's start by reading the whole speech...

Read Acts 20:13-38

Prologue

Read Acts 20:13-16

This is the only time that most of these places appear in the Bible. Troas, Assos and Miletus were on the mainland, while Mitylene, Chios and Samos were islands just off the coast of Asia Minor.

- ❓ Roughly how long did this trip take in total?
- ❓ Why was Paul in such a hurry (v 16)?

Paul's ministry

Miletus was over 50 miles south of Ephesus. But before heading home Paul had something to say to the Ephesian elders.

Read Acts 20:17-21

- ❓ What three descriptions marked Paul's service to the Lord (v 19)?
- ❓ What did Paul engage in (v 20-21)?
- ❓ What was the twofold message he declared (v 22)?
- ❓ What is the significance of the first two words of Paul's address, "You know" (v 18, repeated in v 20)?

TIME OUT

❓ Think about Jesus. Can you think of any stories from his life where the same three descriptions in verse 19—humility, tears, severe testing—applied to him?

Apply

- ❓ In times of severe testing, have you continued to serve Jesus with humility and tears?
- ❓ Is humility something you need to pray about and work on?

No matter how you answer these questions, pause for a moment and give thanks for Jesus, our righteousness, whose perfect service to God covers every deficiency in ours.

Paul's future

Read Acts 20:22-24

- ❓ Why was Paul determined to go to Jerusalem (v 22)?
- ❓ What awaited him there (v 23)?
- ❓ How could he face this prospect and still move towards it (v 24)?

Pray

Is there something hard the Spirit is compelling you to do? Ask him for guidance and courage to do the work he's given you to do.

Bible in a year: Numbers 5 – 8

Paul and the elders, part 2

Paul pivots from what awaits him in Jerusalem to what awaits the elders—and how they should live in response to it. His words are as relevant today as then.

The charge
Read Acts 20:25-27

Paul speaks of being "innocent of the blood" of others (v 26; see 18:6). The image goes back to Ezekiel's call to be a watchman for the people of Israel. **Read Ezekiel 33:1-9** for more detail.

Read Acts 20:28

❓ *What two charges did Paul give them?*

Paul told the "elders" of the church (v 17) that, since the Holy Spirit had made them "overseers" they were to be "shepherds" of God's sheep (v 28). These three terms describe the various roles church leaders play.

❓ *What does each one tell us about what God wants leadership of his people to look like?*

🔼 Pray

Pray for the leaders of your church. Ask that God would empower them to be the elders, overseers and shepherds that he has called them to be, so that the good news about Jesus would spread through your neighbourhood and region.

The warning
Read Acts 20:29-31

❓ *What dangers awaited these churches:*
• *externally (v 29)?* • *internally (v 30)?*

❓ *How should the elders respond (v 31)?*

The power
Read Acts 20:32-35

Paul was committing them to a greater power than himself—"to God and to the word of his grace" (v 32). The assistance God gives us to fulfil our calling is personal (God himself), verbal (his word) and experiential (his enabling grace).

❓ *What did Paul teach the elders by his example (v 35)?*

🔽 Apply

❓ *Who in your church is currently in a situation of weakness? How will you "give" to them?*

The parting
Read Acts 20:36-38

❓ *What does their affection tell you about the relationship between Paul and these elders?*

🔼 Pray

Give thanks that this is the kind of relationship you can enjoy with brothers and sisters. Pray that you would continue to enjoy, or be given opportunities to begin to enjoy, this gospel-grounded closeness within your church.

Bible in a year: 1 Chronicles 10 – 14

Prophets and prophecy

Of the gifts listed in Ephesians 4:11 which are given to build up his church—apostles, prophets, evangelists, pastors, teachers—perhaps the least familiar is the prophet.

In both the Old and New Testaments, prophets had a God-given ability both to predict the future and to proclaim God's message. No story in the New Testament gives us a better window into this gift than today's.

Through the Spirit

Read Acts 21:1-6

❷ *What message did the believers in Tyre have for Paul (v 4)?*

❷ *From whom did they receive this message (v 4)?*

"Through the Spirit" indicates that some disciples in Tyre had the gift of prophecy. Elsewhere, Paul gave instructions for how believers are to receive prophetic messages—**read 1 Thessalonians 5:19-22.**

❷ *Did he follow his own advice?*

The Holy Spirit says…

Read Acts 21:7-9

While Christians differ over precisely how it should work in practice, there is no doubt that the New Testament celebrates the ministry of women in the church, and the speaking role of women within church gatherings (see 1 Corinthians 11:5).

❷ *What Spirit-filled women speak God's word to you? Take a moment to send them a message to thank them for their ministry to you and to your church.*

Read Acts 21:10-11

OT prophets used object lessons to make their point (e.g. Jeremiah 27:2; Ezekiel 4:1).

❷ *What symbol did Agabus use?*

❷ *What point did he convey?*

The Lord's will be done

Read Acts 21:12-16

It might sound as though Paul's determination to go to Jerusalem contradicted what the Holy Spirit wanted (v 4)—or worse, that the Spirit was contradicting himself (compare verse 4 to 20:22). When handling prophecy, we must differentiate three distinct elements: the prediction itself, the exhortation based on the prediction, and the response to both the prediction and the exhortation.

❷ *What was the prediction (21:11)?*

❷ *What was the exhortation based on the prediction (v 12)?*

❷ *What was Paul's response to the exhortation (v 13)? What was Paul's response to the prediction?*

▲ Pray

It is humbling to realise that, though we may hear God's word clearly, we may still misunderstand or misapply what he is saying. Ask the Spirit for humility to hear his words and to put them into practice as he wants.

Bible in a year: Psalm 99 – 101

Acts 21:17-26

Planning and opposition

Paul went to Jerusalem "not knowing what [would] happen to [him] there" (Acts 20:22). The elders there wondered the exact same thing!

Report

Read Acts 21:17-19

This James is not the apostle, who was martyred by Herod Agrippa I (12:2). This is James the half-brother of Jesus (Mark 6:3; Galatians 1:19), a leading elder of the Jerusalem church (Acts 15:13), and the author of the epistle bearing his name (James 1:1).

❷ *If you had to give a ten-word report on what God had done among the Gentiles through Paul, what would you say?*

Recommendation

Read Acts 21:20-26

❷ *How had the Jerusalem church been doing while Paul had been away in Gentile lands (v 20)?*

❷ *What conclusion had the new Jewish believers reached concerning Paul (v 21)?*

❷ *What concern did the elders have about this conclusion (v 24)?*

❷ *What course of action did they recommend Paul take (v 23-24)?*

Stories like this remind us that we have the freedom and the obligation to "contextualise" the message of Jesus—to *shape* our words and actions in ways that are both appropriate to the culture and subversive of its idolatries, while ensuring that we do not *change* the gospel. In this case what Paul does (likely a Nazirite vow, see Numbers 6:1-21) signals that believers are free to follow Jewish cultural norms, while also asserting that these actions do not save.

Believers often disagree about contextualisation. Some think the church is going too far, others that it's not going far enough. This story reminds us that everyone—even Paul—needs others to help them discern the right path forward.

Apply

❷ *If you were to err in one direction or the other, would it be towards not shaping the gospel so that it can be heard well or towards not being clear on the gospel so that it is not heard at all? In other words, are you more tempted to ignore culture or copy culture?*

❷ *What would a contextualised but unchanged gospel explanation sound like in your particular context?*

Pray

Don't miss the fact that this passage shows that established churches can be effective in evangelism. No matter how old your church is, ask the Lord to empower your witness so that more people may come to know the love of Jesus.

Bible in a year: Proverbs 19

That didn't work…

"Everybody has a plan," the boxer Mike Tyson said, "till they get punched in the mouth". In a sense this proved literally true for Paul. Yet in another, it all went exactly to plan.

Beaten
Read Acts 21:27-32

- What four charges were brought against Paul (v 28)?
- What did the mob do to Paul (v 27, 30, 31, 32)?
- What prevented them from killing him (v 32)?

Just because we seek the input of others doesn't mean things will turn out the way we want. The elders gave Paul wise counsel (v 23-24), but it didn't prevent trouble from befalling him.

Pray

When we're suffering, it's natural to wonder where we went wrong. Sometimes, however, suffering is simply part of God's plan for us (see 1 Peter 4:12).

Ask God to help you endure whatever suffering you face, to relieve you of any false guilt and to help you experience it as a "participation in [Christ's] sufferings, becoming like him in his death" (Philippians 3:10). Then pray the same for friends and family who are hurting.

Arrested
Read Acts 21:32-36

Note the word "ran" (v 32). No doubt the commander had many reasons for getting there quickly—to stop things from getting out of hand, to avoid being charged with rioting (see 19:40), to assert his control. Whatever his motivation, the effect was that Paul's life was spared (21:31-32). God works through people who don't even know him to accomplish his will.

Faithful
Read Acts 21:37-40

- What surprised the commander about Paul (v 37)?
- Who did he think Paul was (v 38)?
- What did Paul want to do (v 40)?

Even at his lowest moment—beaten, bloodied, chained—Paul was an opportunist for the good news about Jesus.

- Read Romans 5:1-5; 12:19-21. Where did this love for his opponents come from?

Pray

Ask God to give you such love for Jesus and such a heart for others that you become an opportunist for the gospel, especially when things don't seem to go according to plan.

Bible in a year: Hosea 1 – 7

Paul's first defence

Paul now gives a lengthy defence—the first of many such speeches recorded in Acts. Each time, as we'll see, he chooses his words carefully, to have maximum impact.

Backstory

Read Acts 22:1-5

- What had been Paul's relationship to the Law of Moses (v 3)?
- How did Paul describe his mistreatment of Jesus' disciples (v 4-5)?

For his "defence" (v 1) Paul told the story of his own transformation from being "as zealous for God as any of you" (v 3) as a Jew, to becoming a follower of Jesus.

- Why do you think Paul chose his personal story instead of a logical argument?
- What did he hope to gain by sharing this backstory, do you think?

Conversion

Read Acts 22:6-9

- According to verse 4, who had Paul been persecuting?
- According to verses 7-8, who had Paul been persecuting?

In his letters Paul gave a series of analogies describing the profound connection between Christ and his church. It is like a foundation and a building (1 Corinthians 3:10-11), a head and a body (Ephesians 4:15-16), a husband and a wife (5:21-32).

- How do these pictures shed light on our union with Jesus?

Read Acts 22:10-13

- What was Ananias' relationship to the Law of Moses (v 12)? Why do you think Paul pointed this out in this speech?

Calling

Read Acts 22:14-16

- God chose Paul to do four things (v 14-15). What are they?
- Before he could get on with his calling, what did Paul need to do first (v 16)?

Apply

- What is your story of finding Jesus? Use the section headings from this study to help you write it down. It is a powerful witness to Jesus to share where you were, how you were turned around and where God by his grace has brought you.

Read Acts 22:17-21

This story occurred when Paul returned to Jerusalem immediately after his conversion (see 9:26).

- Where did Paul want to testify to the good news about Jesus? Why?
- Where was he called to go instead?

It's okay to tell God what you would like and why. But at the end of the day Jesus is our Lord not our waiter, and we must trust him with his calling in our lives.

- What has he given you to do today? What will it look like to get on with it?

Bible in a year: John 7 – 9

Great King, great hope

This is a royal psalm, celebrating and praying for God's grace in the king's life and rule. It is a psalm about Solomon, but its details cause us to look beyond Solomon...

... and to discover another—the King of all the nations.

Apply

- *The world is cynical about power. How should Christians relate to human power and to God's power, do you think?*
- *"God reigns." Does this sound like good news to you? If it does, how would you explain to someone else why that is good news?*

Limitless power

Read Psalm 72

This king is the judge and defender of his people (v 2-4). His rule will have no limits, either across the nations or throughout time (v 7-8). The nations will see his glory, and know that he is their rightful king (v 9-11, 15, 17). His kingdom will be one of plenty (v 15-16).

Boundless love

No one wants a king who is aloof and indifferent to the real needs of his people. Who wants to be ruled by someone preoccupied by the privileges of wealth and power? Happily, this king is the exact opposite of self-aggrandisement. This king is a king of love. His rule will be one of love, compassion and kindness (v 4, 12-14).

Apply

- *Which is your favourite aspect of the king's rule in these verses?*
- *How does this king show mercy to the weak (v 12-14)?*
- *Read Galatians 6:2 and James 1:27. How will you do likewise?*

Glorious hope

Did these prayers find their answer in Solomon's day? Israel never enjoyed more peace and wealth before or after Solomon, and his wisdom fills books of the Bible. But the prayers of the psalm are only being realised now, in the advancing kingdom of Jesus. As Jesus said, "Now one greater than Solomon is here" (Matthew 12:42, NIV84). It is Jesus' kingdom that shall endure for ever, Jesus' glory that is filling the earth, and the glory of his love that brings healing, joy and hope. This psalm is your signpost to the blessings he brings, and his invitation to taste the delights of belonging to him and to his kingdom.

Apply

- *"Behold your King," said Pontius Pilate (John 19:14, ESV). Will you?*

Pray

Read **Psalm 72:18-19** and use it to shape your praise and your prayers today.

Bible in a year: 2 Timothy 1 – 2

A Roman citizen

Like Stephen (Acts 7:54), Paul was unable to finish his defence because the crowd had had enough. And it looks as if Paul will meet the same fate as Stephen did...

Interruption

Read Acts 22:22

What was significant about the crowd stopping Paul at this point in his defence?

- ❷ Think about it this way: what would it have said about the mob if they had stopped him...
  - after he said "as zealous for God as any of you are" (v 3)?
  - after he said "Jesus of Nazareth" (v 8)?
  - after he said "be baptised" (v 16)?

It appears that there was a fierce pride in being the people of God, of being different and better—one that could not abide the thought that in fact God's blessings were just as available to the Gentiles as the Jews, and that the Jews deserved favoured status before God no more than the Gentiles.

Apply

- ❷ Is there any pride in you about being a Christian, that causes you to look down on others who you consider less good—or even, perhaps, less worthy—than you?

Appeal

Read Acts 22:23-25

As you can tell by Paul's question, the answer was no—while it was fine to flog a Jew, it was not legal to flog a Roman citizen without a trial.

Alarm

Read Acts 22:26-29

- ❷ What was different about Paul's citizenship (v 28)?
- ❷ How did the interrogators respond to his statement (v 29)?
- ❷ What about the commander?

We'll never know whether Paul planned to invoke his Roman citizenship before this moment. But we do know that Jesus gave him—and us—a promise. **Read Luke 12:11-12** to see what it is.

Apply

We may think to ourselves, "I don't know how I could manage in that kind of situation".

- ❷ How does Luke 12:11-12 encourage you?
- ❷ Are there situations in your own life where you need to ask the Spirit to give you the right words, and prayerfully open your mouth and see what he prompts you to say?

Pray

Today there will be believers being hauled before judges and soldiers simply because they know Jesus. Pray now that the Spirit will give them faith, courage—and words.

Bible in a year: Numbers 9 – 12

Paul's second defence

Paul's second defence is much shorter than his first. This time, he only manages to get out three sentences…

An unforced error

Read Acts 22:30 – 23:5

- ❓ *Read Matthew 23:27-28. What did Paul mean when he called the high priest a "whitewashed wall" (Acts 23:5)?*

How could Paul not have recognised who the high priest was? It could be due to his poor eyesight (see Galatians 4:15; 6:11), his long absence from Jerusalem or simply his surprise that the high priest would order someone to be struck. Whatever the reason, Paul's trial before the Sanhedrin got off on the wrong foot.

A shrewd reframing

Read Acts 23:6-9

- ❓ *Paul makes three assertions in verse 6. What are they?*

Remember the four original charges brought against Paul (21:28)?

- ❓ *In what way(s) did each of them relate to Paul's assertion in 23:6?*
- ❓ *What was the response to his statement?*

This was a remarkably shrewd move by Paul. Not only did he instantly win defenders to his side—remarkably, the Pharisees!—he also reframed the debate. No longer would the key issue be whether people should observe Jewish customs. From now on, the conversation would centre on the resurrection.

There is a lesson in this for us too. We may not be appearing before Jewish religious leaders to defend the gospel. But wherever we are able to talk about our faith, it is good to move the conversation towards the resurrection, for that is the historical rock on which the truth of the gospel stands or falls but also the place that declares that eternal life is available.

🔼 Pray

Pray for greater insight into Jesus' resurrection so that you can increasingly reframe anything in life from that perspective.

An unexpected command

Read Acts 23:10-11

- ❓ *How do you think this command (v 11) would have affected Paul emotionally and spiritually?*

🔽 Apply

We may not know the specifics regarding where we will go or how much longer we will live. But God has given us a book full of promises.

- ❓ *What are your favourite promises from God?*
- ❓ *What would be different about the way you live today if you had no doubt he would fulfil them?*

Bible in a year: 1 Chronicles 15 – 19

Overheard

As soon as Jesus promised Paul he'd testify in Rome, a conspiracy formed to end his life before he got anywhere near the capital. How would the Lord fulfil his promise?

The plot made
Read Acts 23:12-15

- ❓ *How long did the conspirators think it would take to fulfil their vow (v 12, 20)?*
- ❓ *What was their reason for conspiring against Paul (21:28)?*

TIME OUT

There is a parallel story to this in the Old Testament, when King Joram of Israel vows to kill the prophet Elisha before the end of the day—**read 2 Kings 6:30-31**. Threats like these were by no means empty. Read the prayers of Elijah (1 Kings 19:14) and Nehemiah (Nehemiah 9:26).

- ❓ *How did Jesus describe the city of Jerusalem (Luke 13:34)?*

Those who speak God's word are in constant danger of upsetting powerful people. Not every season in every place is rife with persecution and martyrdom; Jerusalem did not murder a prophet every year. Still, the good news about Jesus speaks of human fallenness, redemption through death, and a resurrected King: an unpopular message in the best of times and a dangerous one in the worst.

▲ Pray

Pray for Christians who are called to witness to the truth in places where persecution is to be expected and martyrdom is not uncommon. Pray that you, too, in a situation that will be less dangerous than that, will be given courage to stand for Jesus. Pray for an opportunity to do so today.

The plot foiled
Read Acts 23:16-22

- ❓ *Why does the plot start to unravel?*

When we think about the role of God in our lives, it's helpful to differentiate between primary and secondary causes. For example, the Bible promises that God will provide everything I need (Matthew 6:25-34). I have a job that provides for my family. So why do I have what I need—God or my job? The answer, of course, is both. God is the primary cause, the reason behind every other reason for what happens in life (Genesis 45:5-8). My job is the secondary cause, the instrument by which God fulfils his promise to me (Proverbs 13:4). Why was Paul's life spared? Paul's nephew is the secondary cause—God's promise is the primary.

▲ Pray

We are called, having prayed, to be "watchful and thankful" for the ways that God answers our prayers (Colossians 4:2). Ask God to encourage you by giving you eyes to see some of how he is working in your life today—including through secondary causes.

Bible in a year: Psalm 102 – 104

Under cover of night

Over 40 men lay in ambush, hungry and thirsty and murderous. Could Paul escape Jerusalem?

A detachment

Read Acts 23:23-24

The entire garrison in Jerusalem consisted of 1,000 soldiers.

> How many of them did the commander send to protect Paul (v 23)?

Sometimes we justify inaction by appealing to faith: "I'm not going to do anything; God will handle this". At other times we try to make things happen all by ourselves and neglect to pray. These two verses show how harmonious primary and secondary causes really are. God fulfilled his promise to protect Paul by providing nearly 500 soldiers to guard him on his way! The Lord doesn't need secondary causes to accomplish his purposes, but he normally uses them.

Apply

> Are you more prone to hold back from doing things or to move forwards without praying?

> What would it look like in your life to balance prayer and action?

A letter

Read Acts 23:25-30

> Based on what he'd heard, what was the commander's verdict (v 29)?

> Why did he send Paul to the governor (v 30)?

Marcus Antonius Felix was born into slavery but later freed by Antonia, the mother of Emperor Claudius. Felix gained influence in Rome, ultimately becoming the procurator (governor) of Judea. Tacitus wrote of him, "With all cruelty and lust he exercised the power of a king with the spirit of a slave".

An introduction

We've encountered Caesarea as a point of transit for Paul. Herod the Great (see Matthew 2) built Caesarea into a flourishing city. By the time of this story, it was the largest city in Judea, with a multiethnic population. Under Felix, tensions boiled over between Jews and Syrians in Caesarea.

Read Acts 23:31-35

> Is Paul in a better position now than earlier in Acts 23, do you think? Why/why not?

> What does Paul now need to wait for?

Pray

Sometimes God simply calls us to wait, and like Paul we don't know for how long. But as the hymnwriter said, "His purposes will ripen fast, unfolding every hour".

Ask him to give you patience as you await the unfolding of his will, and faith to continue following—especially in areas where you would like quicker answers or more obvious ways forward.

Bible in a year: Proverbs 20 – 21

Paul's third defence

What parts of your life do you view as being valuable for the kingdom? Which seem comparatively mundane or even useless? This story may hold a surprise for you.

The case against Paul

This long story has multiple groups of actors. It'll help make sense of today's reading to review the part each group played.

- Jews from the province of Asia (21:27-28)
- The crowd in Jerusalem (21:30; 22:22-23)
- The chief priests and the Sanhedrin (22:30)
- The conspirators (23:12-14)

Read Acts 24:1-8

❓ *Who travelled to Caesarea for the trial (v 1)?*

❓ *What three charges does Tertullus level against Paul (v 5-6)?*

☑ Apply

One reason God forbids "bear[ing] false witness" and not simply "lying" (Exodus 20:16, KJV) is that we are capable of stringing true statements together to create a false impression.

❓ *In what situations or relationships are you most likely to shade the truth for personal benefit?*

The case for the defence

Read Acts 24:9-16

❓ *How does Paul respond to each charge Tertullus brought against him (v 11-13)?*

❓ *Paul describes his life in five ways (v 14-16). What are they?*

Unlike his first two defences (22:1-21; 23:1-6), for the first time Paul offers a kind of personal creed.

❓ *What do you think Paul hoped to accomplish with this tactic?*

Faith in Jesus Christ is not a departure from but rather the fulfilment of the Hebrew Scriptures (Acts 24:14). We can read the Old Testament with confidence that all of it ultimately brings us to the Lord Jesus Christ.

Read Acts 24:17-21

The charges that Tertullus had brought up originated with Jews from the province of Asia. But they were not present. Therefore, Paul argued, the only relevant charge for this trial was the one that the chief priests and the Sanhedrin did hear—the resurrection of the dead (v 21).

☑ Apply

Paul used every tool he had—his knowledge of the Scriptures, his rights as a Roman citizen, his extensive education, his ability to reason, his courtroom savvy—to defend himself. God is at work in every part of your life, even in what seems mundane or "unspiritual". No one is wise enough to know what they will need or not need. But God is, and he's forming each part of your journey to make you the person he's called you to be.

Bible in a year: Hosea 8 – 14

Waiting for Felix

Rather than exploring this passage one section at a time, we're going to read the whole thing first, and then trace different threads running through the story.

Read Acts 24:22-27

Felix

Drusilla (v 24) was Felix's second wife. She was of noble birth. Her father was Herod Agrippa I, whom we met in Acts 12:1-4, and her brother was Herod Agrippa II, who appears in the next chapter.

Luke points out that Felix "was well acquainted with the Way" (24:22).

❓ *How might his familiarity with the good news have affected the way Paul shared Jesus with him?*

Apply

❓ *When you talk with others about Jesus, how does their comparative familiarity or unfamiliarity with the gospel affect the way you talk about Jesus?*

Felix and Paul

❓ *How often did Felix and Paul converse (v 26)?*

❓ *What four themes did Paul highlight with Felix (v 24-25)?*

❓ *Given what you know of Felix, why do you think Paul chose these topics?*

···· TIME OUT ····································

So what would Paul have said about these topics? Here's what he wrote about them:

- Faith in Christ Jesus: Galatians 3:7-14
- Righteousness: Romans 3:21-28
- Self-control: Titus 2:6-8, 11-14
- The judgment to come: Romans 2:5-6

Apply

Sharing Jesus with others can be intimidating: "What if they ask me a question I cannot answer?" No one is entirely prepared, but one way to lessen this concern is the very thing you're doing right now—regularly reading and studying the Scriptures. The Holy Spirit has a remarkable way of connecting your personal meditation on the word with the people you encounter day by day. Trust him; he might surprise you!

Paul's plight

❓ *When did Felix say he would decide Paul's case (Acts 24:22)?*

❓ *How did Felix treat Paul (v 23)?*

❓ *Why did Felix delay his decision? (There are two reasons, one in verse 26 and one in verse 27.)*

❓ *How long was Paul imprisoned for (v 27)?*

Pray

One of the most difficult things God asks us to do is wait. Take a moment to pray the words of Psalm 42 as an expression of your faith while you await his leading.

Bible in a year: John 10 – 12

Is it really worth it?

Most of us wonder sometimes: is being a Christian really worth it? Wouldn't it be easier and better to be like everyone else? This psalm was written for those moments.

Okay, but… really?
Read Psalm 73:1

Every member of God's people knows the theory—God is good to his people. Verse 1 is true. The problem is that sometimes the evidence of our eyes and the feelings of our hearts say, "No it isn't!"

On the verge
Read Psalm 73:2-14

How does the writer, Asaph, describe the state of his faith and his view of living for God (v 2, 13-14)?

❓ *Why is he feeling like this (v 3-12)?*

If God is good to his people, why do his people find life so hard? Why do others have life so easy, when they spend their easy lives mocking God? If you find yourself surrounded by those to whom God seems to have given far more than you, and yet who mention him only to laugh about him, then you are not the first. Asaph knew what this was like. And it had caused him to think seriously about abandoning his faith and joining the world. The grass there just looked so green.

In the sanctuary
Read Psalm 73:15-28

But he can't quite do it. There's something about the impact it would have on his godly friends ("your children") that makes him hold back. And so he's torn apart (v 16)…

❓ *… until he goes where and understands what (v 17)?*

The sanctuary was the heart of God's temple in Jerusalem. Its existence spoke of the truth that God is present in this world, and that he is the Lord of eternity.

❓ *So what did he realise about the prosperous, popular God-mocking people of verses 3-12 (v 18-20)?*

❓ *What did he realise about himself, even when he's acting like a "brute beast" in his confusion (v 23-26)?*

Asaph realised this great truth: it's not the journey that matters; it's the destination. A hard road to glory is infinitely and eternally better than a first-class ticket to hell. The grass is not greener there. It is dead.

▼ Apply

❓ *How will you look at the best things in your life, the worst things in your life, and the people around you who have everything you'd like in your life…*
 • *if you forget eternal reality?*
 • *if you remember eternal reality?*

❓ *What would change if you said to yourself every morning, "He has taken hold of me… he is guiding me… he will take me to his glory"?*

Bible in a year: 2 Timothy 3 – 4

Paul's fourth defence

Two years: that's how long Paul waited in a Caesarean prison. That's how long Paul waited for God's promise to come to pass (Acts 23:11).

Now it was time to make it happen.

Accusations

Felix's tenure as procurator ended when tensions between Jewish and Syrian citizens of Caesarea boiled over and Felix employed harsh measures to quell the riots. After the citizens appealed to Rome, Nero recalled Felix and installed Porcius Festus in his place.

Read Acts 25:1-5

❶ What did the chief priests and leaders want Festus to do (v 3)? Why?

❶ What did Festus decide to do (v 5)?

Read Acts 25:6-7

❶ How does Luke characterise the charges levelled against Paul (v 7)? What problem did the prosecution have?

🔺 Pray

False accusations inspire us to ask God to vindicate us. **Read Psalm 43** and consider what comfort it would have brought Paul in this moment. But there was another who prayed this psalm of vindication. **Reread Psalm 43** as a prayer of Jesus.

❶ At what point(s) of his earthly life would this psalm have been timely?

Now pray this psalm for yourself, as one united to Jesus. Ask that, amid false accusation, God would fill your mouth with praise and your heart with hope.

Defence before Festus

Read Acts 25:8-9

❶ Where did Festus want to reconvene the trial?

❶ Before whom would Paul have been tried?

Read Acts 25:10-12

❶ What objections did Paul raise to this plan?

❶ To whom did Paul appeal?

After waiting two years, Paul was ready to go to Rome, and he used the right of *provocatio* to do it. This privilege for Roman citizens went back two centuries to the Porcian Law. If the word Porcian looks familiar, that's because it is the ancestral clan of this new procurator, Porcius Festus!

Paul could have invoked this right in his conversations with Felix but chose not to, perhaps because he didn't trust Felix to fulfil his request. But Paul knew Festus would regard *provocatio* as an ancestral gift from his family to Roman citizens everywhere. Festus was far more likely to grant Paul's request—and he did (v 12).

🔺 Pray

Ask for resourcefulness to use everything at your disposal to advance God's purposes in your life.

Bible in a year: Numbers 13 – 16

I'd like to hear him myself

Festus has granted Paul's appeal to Caesar (v 11-12). The apostle could not have anticipated having to make yet another defence before he got to Rome. But he will…

Conferral

Read Acts 25:13-15

Luke introduces two more Roman nobles, Herod Agrippa II and his sister Bernice. (Another sibling, Drusilla, was Felix's second wife.) The relationship between procurators like Festus and kings like Agrippa is not always clear. But part of Agrippa's responsibility was the jurisdiction of the temple; in that role he named the high priest. So he was quite familiar with the situation in Jerusalem. That familiarity made him a good conversation partner for Festus.

Read Acts 25:16-22

❓ What did the religious authorities want Festus to do (v 15)?

❓ What surprised Festus about their charges (v 19)?

❓ In his second defence, what theological issue had Paul said was the point of contention (23:6)?

❓ What new information about this theological issue did Festus raise (25:19)?

Interview

The resulting conversation was less a trial than it was an interview. No one raised charges against Paul, and the procurator had already issued a decision (v 25). At Agrippa's request, however, Festus created a formal opportunity for the king to hear the apostle for himself.

Read Acts 25:23-27

❓ Who was present for this conversation (v 23)?

❓ What did the chief priests and elders want Festus to do (v 24)?

❓ What decision had he reached (v 25)?

❓ Why did he say he arranged the interview with Agrippa (v 26)?

This turn of events must have come as a surprise to Paul.

❓ In the few moments before "Paul was brought in" (v 23), what do you think he prayed?

❓ What promises of God might have been particularly encouraging at this moment?

🔖 Pray

Life rarely goes the way we expect it to, but our Lord is never surprised. What unexpected turns have you faced this week? Ask God for grace to handle the unexpected with hopefulness and courage. Pray that, when things go sideways, the Spirit would give you words and deeds that testify to the life and love of Jesus.

Bible in a year: 1 Chronicles 20 – 24

Wednesday 10 September — Acts 26:1-11

Paul's fifth defence, part 1

We come now to Paul's fifth and final defence in the book of Acts. While they may sound similar, each one presents specific points, tailored for his particular audience.

Permission

Read Acts 26:1-3

❓ Why was Paul glad to present his defence to Agrippa (v 3)?

❓ What did he ask of Agrippa (v 3)?

Paul knew that he was going to Rome, both because of God's promise (23:11) and Festus' decision (25:12).

❓ Since he knew that this interview would not result in his release, what did he hope to accomplish? (Hint: see 26:29.)

Upbringing

Read Acts 26:4-5

❓ If you could select one word from these verses to sum up Paul's upbringing, what would it be?

Read Acts 26:6-8

❓ How many times does Paul use the words "hope" or "promise" in verses 6-7?

❓ What was this hope (v 8)?

The resurrection of Jesus remains a stumbling block to faith. Sceptics assert that it is the unscientific product of a pre-enlightened mind. But ancient peoples were not as credulous as we suppose, as Paul's question (v 8) makes clear. Jesus' resurrection remains the only miracle that ultimately matters. If it didn't happen, then the gospel is nothing. If it did, then it is everything.

Zeal

Read Acts 26:9-11

❓ How many crimes against Christians can you find in these verses?

Zeal in the name of God is not necessarily good. Hatred, indifference or injustice are often justified in the name of religiosity or spirituality.

⮞ Apply

Again, Paul is using his own story to begin to outline the gospel. While you're not called to be an apostle, nor (probably) to defend yourself before a king, you are called to give a reason for the hope you have—and you can do so by sharing the gospel through sharing your story.

❓ So what would you say to someone about...
- your life before you were saved (or before you started to take your faith seriously)?
- what God did to bring you to put your faith in Jesus?
- the difference this made to your life, especially to your hopes and sense of purpose?

❓ Review your answers. Would someone listening gain a sense that Jesus is alive, that he is powerful, that he is loving, and that he forgives?

Bible in a year: Psalm 105 – 107

Acts 26:12-23 — Thursday 11 September

Paul's fifth defence, part 2

Luke continues the story of Paul's interview with Agrippa, where we find the apostle drawing the king's attention to the most significant moment in his life.

Stopped

Read Acts 26:12-14

Paul says he had "the authority and commission of the chief priests" (v 12).

❷ *What weight would this carry with Agrippa?*

Compare verse 14 with Acts 9:4. Though this is the third record of his conversion in Acts, for the first time Paul includes a sentence that Jesus told him.

❷ *What is it?*

A "goad" was a pointy stick used by farmers to keep a stubborn animal moving. No matter how hard the animal kicked, the farmer was going to keep it moving. Thus "to kick against the goads" became a common expression to describe a futile, hopeless task.

Apply

❷ *Can you think of a time when you kicked against the goads? What finally made you give in to the will of God?*

❷ *Do you have any sense that you might be kicking against the goads at the moment?*

Called

Read Acts 26:15-18

Each account of Paul's conversion includes the two sentences: "Why do you persecute me?" and "I am Jesus, whom you are persecuting" (v 14-15; 9:4-5; 22:7-8). So closely does Jesus identify with his people that, by persecuting his people, Paul was persecuting *him*.

❷ *What did God appoint Paul to be (26:16)? What does each term tell us about his calling?*

❷ *For what purpose did God send Paul to Jews and Gentiles (v 18)?*

❷ *What two benefits would people receive through Paul's ministry (v 18)?*

Pray

What grace! Give thanks to God for giving you both the forgiveness of your sins and a place at his table through Christ our Lord.

Seized

Read Acts 26:19-23

❷ *What was the reason why the religious authorities had seized Paul in the temple courts (v 20-21)?*

❷ *What four predictions did Moses and the OT prophets make about the Messiah (v 23)?*

Jesus is "the first to rise from the dead" (v 23)—but not the last! On his return, his people will rise to new life in new bodies too. If you trust Jesus, that includes you!

Bible in a year: Proverbs 22

Friday 12 September — Acts 26:24-32

Do you believe?

STOP! Festus had had enough. Paul's fifth defence was done.

True and reasonable
Read Acts 26:24-25

❓ *What point did Paul make that led Festus to conclude that the apostle was "out of [his] mind" (v 22-23)?*

Paul's first defence had met an untimely interruption too…

❓ *Read 22:19-22. What had Paul said that had led the crowd to shout him down?*

⌄ Apply

The gospel is true, but in order for us to be persuasive we must show how it is also reasonable.

❓ *What pastors or authors have you found who help you see and explain the reasonableness of the Christian faith? In what areas of our faith do you think you could do with some more assistance?*

Not in a corner
Read Acts 26:26-28

❓ *Why did Paul address Agrippa directly (v 26)?*

❓ *What did Paul ask Agrippa if he believed (v 27)?*

❓ *How did Agrippa interpret Paul's question (v 28)? What did he believe Paul was trying to do?*

The apostle's question was shrewd. He didn't ask if Agrippa believed in Jesus as the Messiah or even if he believed in the resurrection. He asked if Agrippa believed the prophets, the basis of his message (v 23). Like the other Herods in his family, Agrippa was a Jewish man who sided with the Romans. But he had treated the Jews more favourably than his predecessors. By phrasing the question this way, Paul put Agrippa in a tight spot. If Agrippa answered "No", he risked the goodwill he had painstakingly earned. But if he said "Yes", Paul would ask him why then he didn't believe the Messiah. That's why Agrippa didn't answer Paul's question, instead deflecting with an incredulous question of his own.

I pray to God
Read Acts 26:29-32

❓ *What did Paul pray for everyone who heard him (v 29)?*

⌃ Pray

As reasonable as our presentation of Jesus may be, we are incapable of creating faith in Jesus. This power belongs to God alone. Ask the Holy Spirit to move in the hearts of those you love who do not know Jesus. Pray that he would give you opportunities to declare the truth of the gospel and reveal its reasonableness—and that as you do, he would go to work in their hearts.

Bible in a year: Joel 1 – 3

Inching along

Finally, after two years of waiting, Paul now seems on the verge of seeing God's promise to send him to Rome be fulfilled (23:11). But the going will prove very slow...

Slow headway

Read Acts 27:1-8

The ship hung close to the southern coast of Asia Minor (v 2-4), then travelled southwest across the Mediterranean to the southern (lee) side of the island of Crete (v 6-8).

- Given that the story uses "we" throughout, who was clearly with Paul?
- Who else accompanied Paul (v 2)?

Aristarchus was from Thessalonica, a city Paul first visited in Acts 17:1-9.

- What had happened to Aristarchus in Ephesus (19:29)?

Once he finally got to Rome, Paul wrote a letter to the Colossians.

- How did he refer to Aristarchus then (Colossians 4:10)?

Apply

- Sometimes progress towards a good, godly goal is slow. What might God be teaching you in those times?

Dangerous sailing

Read Acts 27:9-12

- What word did Paul use to describe a potential voyage from Crete (v 10)?
- Why did they put out to sea, against Paul's advice (v 12)?

Paul modelled an unusual kind of restraint when he advised staying put (v 10). Clearly he was eager to get to Rome (23:11). And yet he displayed remarkable maturity and wisdom, verbalising a warning that restrained how quickly he would reach his goal. Some things are not worth rushing.

Raging storm

The pilot's intention was to stay close to the coast of Crete and land in a better harbour to the west. It wasn't meant to be...

Read Acts 27:13-20

- What did they do in the face of the hurricane force wind (v 15)?
- How did they keep the ship together (v 17)?

It does not end on a happy note: "We finally gave up all hope". But sometimes that's the way life is. It seems that even Paul thought it was over, for reasons we'll consider tomorrow.

Pray

- Do you know anyone who is dangerously close to giving up hope?

Speak to God on their behalf. Ask God to make a way out of no way for them. Then get in contact with them to let them know you love them and are praying for them. Who knows how God might use you in their life?

Bible in a year: John 13 – 15

Our God can

In Psalm 73, Asaph recovers his joyful faith in God by looking forwards. In this psalm, in equally hard times, he recovers his confidence by looking upwards.

Utter defeat

Read Psalm 74:1-8

- What has happened to God's people?
- What is Asaph asking God (v 1)?

Apply

- Why might we wonder about these things today, as we consider the state of the church around the world?
- Why is it liberating to find God's word giving voice to these tensions?

Total silence

Read Psalm 74:9-11

Worse than all of verses 1-8 is verse 9. God's word has fallen silent. In the midst of catastrophe, there seems to be no guidance from God. No prophet has come to say, *It's okay. I'm still here. I'll keep my promises.* And "none of us knows how long this will be" (v 9).

This suggests that this psalm was written in the time of the exile, when the Babylonians had destroyed Jerusalem (Zion), flattened the temple, and taken Judah's political and religious leaders into exile. The prophet Jeremiah had last been seen being dragged towards Egypt. There was nothing left. And the silence left by God was filled with the mockery of God's enemies towards the God who seemed to have forgotten his people.

Apply

- In what (less extreme) sense do we experience verses 9-11 today?

But God

Read Psalm 74:12-23

- What two aspects of God's character does Asaph remember (v 12)?
- How would this comfort him?
- What has God done (v 13-17)?

God can control the seas and God can crush chaos and brutality. God can provide life and God can sustain equilibrium. God can… do anything. So no matter how desperate things look and how silent God seems, he is still the Lord (v 18)—the Creator God who knows his people. He was the King who brought salvation and he still is. And so Asaph prays, still in difficulty but now with a more confident tone. The God who splits seas is the God who can save his people. And for us, we have far clearer knowledge of God to look to. The God who calmed the storm and crushed the grave is the King who still rules, still wins and still saves.

Pray

Tell God how you identify with verses 1-11 as you consider the state of the world and the church. Then thank him that verse 12 is true. Look back at what God has done through Jesus in history, and pray with confidence.

Bible in a year: Titus 1 – 3

Acts 27:21-32 Monday 15 September 77

A messenger of hope

Yesterday we ended with the dark statement, "We finally gave up all hope of being saved"—even Paul, who for years had banked on God's promise to send him to Rome.

How would God reawaken faith in the apostle and, through him, foster faith in the hundreds of other people on board (v 37)?

Keep up your courage

Read Acts 27:21-26

We might hear a hint of "I told you so" in verse 21, but it was important for Paul to affirm his trustworthiness, considering his instructions to the crew.

- What did he exhort everyone to do (v 22, 25)?
- What promise had God given (v 22, 24)?
- How did God assure Paul of this promise (v 23)?

Pray

Paul's testimony in verse 25 shows us that courage comes from faith, and faith rests on God's word. Ask the Lord to give you faith in his word, especially during seasons of darkness, so that you may have courage to follow him and to love your neighbour.

Stay with the ship

Read Acts 27:27-32

Genuine faith always reveals itself in action that matches that faith (see James 2:14-26). If I believe a weather report that promises rain, I'll take an umbrella with me. With this in mind…

- Who believed Paul, and therefore God (Acts 27:32)?
- Who did not believe Paul, and therefore God (v 30)?
- What action proved faith in God (v 32)?

Apply

- Are there areas of your life where your actions (or lack of them) do not match your faith in Jesus?
- What would it look like if you believe his promises, and therefore act in obedience to his commands?

A picture of Jesus

This is the only record of Paul using the phrase, "You cannot be saved" to describe something other than salvation in Jesus (see Acts 16:31; Romans 5:9-10). But this story illustrates the gospel, if you consider the ship as a real-life metaphor depicting Jesus. To be saved we must stay with him (Acts 27:31). But in the process of saving everyone on board (v 24) the ship itself would be crushed (v 22). The only aspect this story couldn't replicate is the resurrection—but the analogy would have been vivid to the survivors.

Pray

- How does viewing this episode in this way move you to praise your Lord Jesus?

Bible in a year: Numbers 17 – 20

Shipwrecked

It was the middle of the night. They'd dropped anchor, dispensed with the lifeboats, and were praying for morning. Their journey was finally coming to an end.

A final meal

Read Acts 27:33-38

- How did Paul describe their two weeks in the storm (v 33)?
- Why did he encourage them to eat (v 34)?
- What promise did he extend to them (v 34)?

Luke's language in verse 35 is reminiscent of the institution of the Lord's Supper (see 1 Corinthians 11:23-24). Clearly Paul was not celebrating Communion on this ship—but as we saw in yesterday's study, the apostle used the moment to illustrate the gospel, and the bread served (at least to Paul and his companions) as a reminder of Jesus' goodness and salvation.

Apply

This is an uncertain world—but Jesus' goodness and sufficiency is certain.

- How are you being called to remember him and give thanks to your Father in difficult circumstances?
- Who do you know who is facing a storm, who you could bring encouragement, perhaps by sharing a meal and the gospel with them?

A final surge

Read Acts 27:39-41

You can sense the desperation.

- By this point, what have the crew discarded (v 18, 19, 32, 38, 40)?

Apply

We, too, will know what it is to be desperate for God to act—where we feel stuck, lacking resources and without hope. We know the "sandy beach" (v 39) that we wish God would enable us to reach—but currently, we are not there. We are, in this sense, on the ship and in the dark. Perhaps this is where you find yourself today.

Read Luke 8:22-25

- How does knowing that Jesus is sovereign over storms, and with you in your storms, give you comfort and encourage your prayers?
- What will it look like for you to live with faith in this moment?

A final threat

Just when you think Paul is safe…

Read Acts 27:42-44

- What did the soldiers want to do (v 42)?
- Who spared Paul's life (v 43)?
- Who reaches the safety of the sandy beach (v 44)?

And so, at last, Paul and his companions reach the shore. God has kept his promise.

Bible in a year: 1 Chronicles 25 – 29

Back on land

Ever had the experience of trying to figure someone out but just not being able to work out who they really are? That's the conundrum for the people of Malta with Paul.

A murderer?

Read Acts 28:1

Malta is an island south of Sicily. The storm has blown them halfway across the Mediterranean—but right on course for their intended destination, Rome!

Read Acts 28:2-4

In Greek mythology Dike ("Justice") was the goddess of moral order, especially in human affairs. The islanders conclude that Paul must have crossed Dike by committing the ultimate crime: murder.

A god?

Read Acts 28:5-6

All along Paul's journey to Rome, we've seen how God often uses secondary causes to accomplish his will—Paul's nephew (23:16), 400+ soldiers (23:23), Roman law (25:11), a storm (27:14). But as Paul's deliverance from a venomous snake proves, God is capable of accomplishing his will apart from natural means too (Luke 10:19).

Pray

Take a moment to ask God to grant healing, provision, restoration—either for yourself or someone you know—either through ordinary or extraordinary means, in a way that brings him glory.

A mistake

The Maltese have found it hard to work Paul out. And their mistakes could have led to serious consequences—either abuse of Paul as a killer, which he was not; or worship of Paul as divine, which he also was not.

An apostle

Read Acts 28:7-10

❓ *How is the presence of the non-divine, non-murderer Paul on Malta a blessing to its inhabitants?*

Throughout Acts we have witnessed the side-by-side nature of words and deeds in gospel ministry—proclamation and action. But this is a rare instance where we find deed ministry (healings) but no record of word ministry (preaching). Perhaps that is because the Maltese did not respond to Paul's message. Or perhaps it is a reminder that acts of mercy and deeds of faith are noteworthy even if and when they do not lead to gospel conversations or conversions. Certainly, knowing Paul as we now do, we can be sure that if there had been an opportunity to share the gospel of Jesus, he would have taken it!

Apply

❓ *In what areas are you called to show Jesus' love? Are you taking opportunities (or making them) to speak of his love?*

Bible in a year: Psalm 108 – 110

Rome, at last!

If I'd been Paul, I think I would have been happy to stay in Malta rather than get back in another boat. But Paul, of course, is on a mission.

Thanksgiving

Read Acts 28:11-14

Syracuse is on the eastern side of Sicily, and Rhegium is on the toe of the boot of Italy. The final leg of their voyage took them to Puteoli, a coastal city south of Rome. From there they travelled on foot.

Read Acts 28:15-16

- How did the believers in Rome show hospitality to Paul (v 15)?
- How did Paul respond (v 15)?

Apply

The hospitality of 1st-century Christians is remarkable (v 14). Hospitality looks different depending on the context.

- What do you think good hospitality means in your context?
- How can you display it?

The plan

Years earlier while Paul was in Corinth (Acts 20:2-3) he'd written a letter to Roman believers whom he'd never met. In it he expressed his hope that this day would come.

- Read Romans 15:23-25, 28-29. When did Paul plan to visit Rome?
- Read Romans 15:30-32. What did Paul ask them to do in the meantime?

Testimony

Read Acts 28:17-20

- Why did Paul say he was in prison (v 20)?

The apostle did not invent the phrase, "the hope of Israel".

Read Jeremiah 14:8; 17:13

- According to the prophet Jeremiah, what is the hope of Israel?

By using a familiar phrase Paul was contextualising his message. He considered his audience's background, beliefs and perspective, and presented the good news in such a way as to gain a hearing and (hopefully) persuade some to believe.

Read Acts 28:21-22

- What had the Jewish leaders heard about Paul (v 21)?
- What had the Jewish leaders heard about the Way (v 22)?

Pray

Ask God to open doors in your area for a clear witness to Jesus. Pray that those you love may have the same eagerness to "hear what your views are" and ultimately come to faith.

Bible in a year: Proverbs 23 - 24

The unfinished story

Schubert's 8th Symphony has two movements instead of the typical four. He began it six years before his death but never finished it. Thus it's called the Unfinished Symphony.

Acts is another masterpiece that, when we reach the ending, feels unfinished.

Persuasion
Read Acts 28:23-24

- What did Paul try to persuade the Jewish leaders about?
- On what basis did he try to persuade them?

TIME OUT

At the end of Luke's first book he quotes Jesus making a similar argument. **Read Luke 24:25-27, 44-45.**

Pray

The "hope of Israel" (Acts 28:20) is Jesus himself. Pray for any Jewish friends and neighbours or those with a "churched" background, that the Holy Spirit would open their hearts to the good news about the Christ who all the Scriptures point to.

Prediction
Read Acts 28:25-27

This is a quotation from Isaiah 6:9-10.

- What was the spiritual condition of Isaiah's hearer—and Paul's (Acts 28:27)?

God spoke this difficult word to Isaiah as part of his call to ministry (Isaiah 6:8). After hearing that his prospects for success were bleak, he understandably asked the Lord, "For how long?" (v 11). This was not a calling anyone would choose.

Apply

Our age is obsessed with success, and it's no different for believers. We applaud leaders with influential ministries and wonder what ordinary pastors with small churches are doing wrong. In reality Jesus is the Lord of the harvest (Luke 10:2), who opens hearts and makes the church grow (1 Corinthians 3:6-7). Like Paul we can learn to become more persuasive (Acts 23:1-6) and contextualise the message (28:17-20), but only God can make our efforts fruitful.

Continuation
Read Acts 28:28-30

- What was the final prediction Paul made in Acts (v 28)?
- Think about the last 2,000 years of human history. Was he right?

The book of Acts ends without a conclusion. It's the unfinished story of Jesus that he continues to write, down through the ages, across languages and cultures, and now through you and me! The Spirit who turned the Roman world upside down is with us! This story is our story and it is... To be continued.

Bible in a year: Amos 1 – 4

Acts, continued

When we began our journey through Acts two issues ago, we identified five themes that Luke weaves throughout the book. We'll take these as our headings for today.

Word and deed

Read Acts 14:1-4

❓ To which are you more inclined: proclamation or action? What about your church? In what ways is the Spirit encouraging you to grow?

Stories of conversion

In the stories of conversion, we saw five marks appear in different combinations: repentance, faith, confessing/calling on the Lord, the gift of the Spirit and baptism.

Read Acts 2:38-41

❓ Think back to your coming to faith in Jesus. Which of these five are part of your story?

Love and community

Read Acts 9:36-39

❓ Who are the Dorcases in your congregation, those whose death would bring great mourning because of all they do? Send them a message, thanking them for their faithful service to Christ.

Opposition and suffering

Read Acts 21:30-32

This is the moment of opposition and suffering that casts its shadow over the rest of the book.

🔼 Pray

Right now throughout the world, believers face this kind of ruthless treatment and unjust imprisonment for the sake of the gospel. Pray that the Spirit would give them courage, faithfulness and hope. Ask that their persecutors, like the Philippian jailer (16:30-31), would come to know Jesus.

Sharing the message

Scan-read Acts 2:14-36

The apostles' teaching included six elements:

- Old Testament prophecy
- The fulfilment of this prophecy in the life, death and resurrection of the Messiah
- Jesus of Nazareth as the Messiah
- The coming of the Holy Spirit
- The future return of Jesus
- Repentance and faith, bringing forgiveness and the Holy Spirit

🔽 Apply

❓ In which of these six areas has your understanding grown the most because of your time in Acts?

❓ How is the Spirit prompting you to be part of the unfinished story of Acts, serving his people and sharing his gospel to the ends of the earth?

Bible in a year: John 16 – 18

LAMENTATIONS: Sorrow

"Those who do not learn from history are bound to repeat it."

Pictures of sorrow

Read Lamentations 1:1

Zion—Jerusalem, the capital of Israel— was once a full city. Now, she is empty. The author uses two analogies to describe her—a wife and a queen.

- ❓ What is the status of the wife now?
- ❓ What has the queen become?
- ❓ Why do you think he chose these analogies?

Causes of sorrow

Lamentations was written in about 575 BC, probably by the prophet Jeremiah. It is a series of meditations on the exile, when God's land was invaded, and God's people were removed to Babylon. The Hebrew title for the book is simply: "How". How did this sorrow come?

Read Lamentations 1:2-7

Jerusalem's "lovers" are absent and her "friends" have betrayed her (v 2).

- ❓ What does "lovers" suggest about her faithfulness as a wife?

Tears are most bitter when they're tears of regret. These people had loved other gods more than the true God. And false gods are no comfort when troubled times come.

- ❓ Who "brought her grief" (v 5)?
- ❓ What is the underlying cause of the invasion, conquest and exile (v 5)?

✅ Apply

- ❓ What do you learn from these verses about looking for love and security outside the Lord?
- ❓ What are the "lovers" you are most tempted by? Why are they so attractive? How will you ensure you resist them?

Read Lamentations 1:8-9

- ❓ How is sin pictured here? What point about sin is being made, do you think?
- ❓ Why do you think not "consider[ing] her future" has (v 9) encouraged Zion to sin?

✅ Apply

- ❓ How seriously do you see your sin?
- ❓ Do verses 8-9 challenge your attitude to it in any way?

Cure for sorrow

Read Lamentations 1:10-11

When friends are enemies (v 2), treasures are gone (v 10), and food is scarce (v 11), all earthly help is gone. All we can do is cry out to God (v 9, 11)—not because we are deserving, but because he is loving.

🙏 Pray

Ask God to use Lamentations to shape your own response to despair in your life. Speak to him now about any issues of which you want to cry, "*Look, Lord!*"

Bible in a year: Philemon

Look!

Jerusalem was an adulterous wife and a treasonous queen. For her unfaithfulness and sin, the Lord let her enemies destroy her.

Looking around

Read Lamentations 1:12-17

Jerusalem now speaks herself, and asks passers-by to see her affliction (v 12).

- ❷ What has become of Jerusalem's strength (v 13-14)?
- ❷ What about...
  - her warriors (v 15)?
  - her children (v 16)?
  - her neighbours (v 17)?

How should a passer-by (another nation or people) respond? With sympathy—Jerusalem has been brought unimaginably low. And with humility—are they (and we) so very different?

We all desire sympathy when we are down. And we are called to show it when others are, too (Romans 12:15). Even if it is a sadness or suffering brought on by sin, Christians can and should still be compassionate—think of our Lord's healing of the high priest's servant's ear (Luke 22:47-51), and kindness to the thief on the cross (Luke 23:40-43).

Apply

- ❷ Is there suffering happening near to you which you are ignoring?
- ❷ Who could you show compassion to today? Will you?

Looking inward

Read Lamentations 1:18

We often respond to suffering with excuses. But Jerusalem offers no excuse. "The LORD is righteous"; yet she is rebellious.

- ❷ What has been placed around Jerusalem's neck, and with what effect (v 14)?
- ❷ If sins brought her suffering, what must occur for her suffering to end?

Looking upward

Read Lamentations 1:19-21

Suffering reveals our weakness. So we cry out to others for help.

- ❷ To what human resources did Zion cry (v 19, 21)? What help did they give?
- ❷ Where does Zion finally turn (v 20-22)?

Pray

When we struggle, we tend to look first to our own resources... then to the help of others... and only then to the Lord of heaven and earth. Ask God to make crying to him your first response to trouble, not your last. And turn to him now, if you need to!

Looking forward

Read Lamentations 1:19-22

The author looks forward to a "day" (v 21) when God will bring justice. How can any sinner want that day to come? **Read Romans 8:33-35.**

Bible in a year: Numbers 21 – 24

Like an enemy

The writer of the letter to the Hebrews warns: "It is a dreadful thing to fall into the hands of the living God" (Hebrews 10:31). Zion's citizens would very much agree.

A great reversal
Read Lamentations 2:1-3

Jerusalem was the most favoured of all cities. Not only was it splendid, it was the place where God had chosen to dwell on earth—his "footstool". But not anymore. The heights of Zion's previous glory are matched by the depths of her dishonour.

- ❷ *What does "daughter" tell us about the relationship between the Lord and Zion?*
- ❷ *What does the Lord's "fierce anger" show us about his concern for what happens on earth?*

··· TIME OUT ···········

Read Jeremiah 7:1-15

The Lord warned the people of Jerusalem to repent. But false prophets told them not to worry, because he would never destroy his temple, never leave his footstool. Too late, the people found out that those were lies. It is a foolish and dangerous thing to ignore the Lord's warnings! **Read 1 Thessalonians 5:1-11.**

The enemy you don't want
Read Lamentations 2:4-5

In the past, the Lord's "right hand"—his infinite power—fought against Israel's enemies. But now, he fights against Israel.

❷ *How do these verses show that we really don't want to have God as our enemy?*

🔺 **Pray**

This is why the angels' announcement at Jesus' birth, that there could now be "peace to those on whom [God's] favour rests" (Luke 2:14), is such wonderful news. The one who we have made into a formidable enemy has reached out to us with an offer of peace.

Confess your sins to God. Admit you deserve his enmity. Thank him for his peace.

Destroyed and rejected
Read Lamentations 2:6-10

As carefully as the Lord had once outlined the building of his house, he now "stretched out a measuring line" (v 8) to measure out his destruction.

❷ *What places, structures, events and people are destroyed?*

This is everything that enables Judah to know relationship and peace with God. Now they are all gone.

🔺 **Pray**

Sin always leads to destruction. It is only because, in this same city, God's Son was trampled, that we can escape it. The destruction of Zion is what we should face. The destruction of Jesus means we don't have to. Thank him now.

Bible in a year: 2 Chronicles 1 – 5

Cry out

Today's reading opens with infants dying in the arms of their mothers. It ends with hints of cannibalism. Such deep suffering requires equally deep hope.

And a glimmer of hope does appear: the people begin to pray.

Sorrow beyond compare
Read Lamentations 2:11-13

The arms of a mother should be a place of safety and nourishment. Yet they are now places of starvation and death.

- ❓ What does the depth of a wound tell you about the healing required?

Failure of false prophets
Read Lamentations 2:14

We saw yesterday that Jerusalem's false prophets scoffed at warnings and calls to repentance.

- ❓ What did the prophets fail to do?
- ❓ Ignoring sin is the opposite of loving someone. But why does it often seem to be unloving to expose sin?

The mocking of enemies
Read Lamentations 2:15-17

What a cruel thing to mock a suffering person. How cruel to mock Jerusalem with their own songs (Psalm 48:2).

- ❓ Who do the enemies claim is responsible for Jerusalem's downfall (Lamentations 2:16)?
- ❓ How does this differ from the author (v 17)?

TIME OUT
Read Matthew 27:41-44

- ❓ How was Jesus' experience similar to that of the people in Lamentations?
- ❓ How does knowing that God's Son went through this encourage us when we suffer greatly?

A call to repentance
Read Lamentations 2:18-19

- ❓ What is the people's response now (v 18)?
- ❓ What response is encouraged (v 19)?

Read Lamentations 2:20-22

These verses record the prayer of the people. They seek the Lord's compassion by highlighting their sorrow. These people have lived through tragedy; and they know that God's hand is behind it all, because of what their hands have done in rebellion against him. So they ask him to "look … and consider" (v 20).

The only one who can heal them is the one who has afflicted them. And the people can know that the Lord does what he plans (v 17). He does punish sin; but he also promises to bless those who turn to him. But to turn truly to him and beg for mercy and restoration, we need first to understand the affliction that our sin leaves us facing.

We need Lamentations, hard though reading these verses is, to remind us what we face if we don't cry out to God for forgiveness.

Bible in a year: Psalm 111 – 113

Where to find hope

Repentance can only come through faith. Faith is stirred by seeing the gracious character of God.

I remember my affliction
Read Lamentations 3:1-17

The author offers a deeply personal account of the affliction he has seen.

- *List the many ways the author has suffered.*

This is a man who has suffered deeply. He is not sitting in an ivory tower, writing tips for people in the real world. He is in the gutter.

He understands that, ultimately, the Lord's hand stands behind this suffering.

- *Where must help and salvation come from?*

Read through these verses a second time. This time, think of how they describe Jesus' experience on the cross.

- *How was Jesus' experience similar?*
- *How was Jesus' experience different?*

… and I am downcast
Read Lamentations 3:18-20

- *How does the writer summarise what has happened to him (v 18)?*
- *How does remembering all this make him feel (v 19-20)?*

Yet I call to mind…
Read Lamentations 3:21-24

He meditates on something that gives him hope, even after (and in) such suffering.

- *Why haven't God's people perished (v 22)?*

Don't miss the force of this. The writer knows that he could (and should) have suffered more. It is only because God is merciful that he's still alive.

Apply

- *How will this idea help and challenge you next time you're going through a really hard time?*

To have hope, we must know who God is. We need to know that our suffering is not beyond his control; and we need to know that he never stops loving his people.

- *What do v 22-23 tell us about who God is?*
- *What does the writer tell himself in v 24?*
- *What does he resolve to do?*

Essentially, he says, *The Lord is all I have, but the Lord is all I need. I will trust him and his timing.*

- *Why is this a liberating way to live?*

His circumstances haven't changed. But his focus has.

Apply

When we struggle with illness, loss, disappointment or sin, we too can think about Jesus and say, "The Lord Jesus is my portion. He is all I need. He has died and risen so that I will never be consumed. He loves me."

Bible in a year: Proverbs 25

What Jesus went through

Yesterday, we ended by meditating on the Lord's love and faithfulness. These are our only hope. Today, we see how meditating on who God is will cause us to respond.

The Lord is good

Read Lamentations 3:25-30

❓ *Who is the Lord good to (v 25)?*

Anyone can say, "When I can see that God is good to me, then I'll follow him". Faith is saying, "I will follow God, and trust him to be good to me".

❓ *What do you think it means to "[seek] him" and "wait quietly" for God's salvation?*

We naturally see suffering as a bad thing, to be avoided. But verses 27-29 give a different perspective. Suffering is a course in patience, faith, and God-centred hope. We should not refuse it or seek revenge in it (v 30).

Apply

❓ *When are you most tempted to seek to "get even"? What would it look like to turn the other cheek to that person?*

The Lord is just

Read Lamentations 3:31-36

The Lord's desire is not to afflict but to love his people.

❓ *Does this mean his people can expect never to suffer (v 32)? What does it mean we can know, then (v 31-32)?*

Verse 33 seems strange, given that Lamentations is a book full of God-given affliction! The point is that our Father does not enjoy watching his people suffer. But, like an earthly father, he is willing to allow us to—or even to cause us to—when he knows that it will bring us back to trusting and hoping in him.

And, though he may use injustice to help us grow in faith and love, those injustices do not go unnoticed (v 34-36).

❓ *How would these verses have given God's people, in exile in Babylon, hope?*

The Lord is Lord

Read Lamentations 3:37-39

❓ *Who is in charge, and of what (v 37-38)?*

❓ *What does no one have the right to do (v 39)?*

Read Lamentations 3:40-47

Living after Jesus, we can know (unlike the writer of Lamentations) that he has been punished for our sins (v 39)—so that we are never "not forgiven" (v 42). He was slain for our sins (v 43). It is very easy to say that Jesus has taken the penalty for our sins— passages like this one remind us of just what we mean by that.

Pray

Reread verses 42-47, thanking God that ultimately this need never be true of us, because it was true of the Lord Jesus. Thank him with all your heart for standing where you should stand, and suffering what you should suffer.

Bible in a year: Amos 5 – 9

Lamentations 3:48-66 — Saturday 27 September

Tears and prayers

Knowledge of our future salvation does not diminish our present pain. And having expressed his hope, the writer of Lamentations returns to his tears.

Continued grief
Read Lamentations 3:48-51

Though the writer is confident of future hope, the present destruction continues. He will weep until the Lord sees and acts. His heart is filled with compassion for the suffering women in his city.

- Does hoping in God's grace bring immediate relief to pain?
- When should our prayers for help end (v 49-50)?

Apply
- How do these verses…
  - give us a reality check about the Christian life?
  - help us not to become disillusioned as we follow Jesus?
- Which do you need more today?

Pray
- About what thing(s) do you need to persevere in prayer today? Now would be a great time!

Unjust justice
Read Lamentations 3:52-54

The Lord used nations to afflict his people for their sin. But now we read they were enemies "without cause" (v 52). The Lord had a reason to afflict them—he was just. Yet these nations had no cause to afflict Israel—they were unjust. This is helpful. We are to look for God's hand when we face difficulty at the hands of others. What is he teaching us? How is he shaping us to rely on him? But we don't need to deny our hurt or our desire for justice.

Our help in ages past
Read Lamentations 3:55-58

- How did the Lord previously respond to the writer's prayers?
- Why is it crucial that he remembers this now, do you think?

Our help right now!
Read Lamentations 3:59-66

- What has the Lord seen and heard (v 59-63)?
- Think back to what the writer has suffered. Why are verses 64-66 reasonable?
- What's the link between verses 55-58 and verses 59-66, do you think?

We've seen two sources of hope in chapter 3: who the Lord is and what he has done.

Pray

Think back to a time when God has answered your prayers. Think further back to the day when he raised his Son. Let them fuel your prayers today.

Bible in a year: John 19 – 21

Complacency costs lives

"If you think you are standing firm, be careful that you don't fall!" (1 Corinthians 10:12).

Who would think…?

Read Lamentations 4:12

- What reputation did Jerusalem have?
- What danger would enjoying such a reputation pose, do you think? (1 Corinthians 10:12 is helpful!)
- Why would Jerusalem's downfall have been shocking?

How the mighty fall

Read Lamentations 4:1-5, 7-8, 10

These verses, which describe a real event, are not easy to read (especially verse 10). The temple's precious stones are scattered in the streets (v 1). Children, more precious than gold, are crushed like common clay (v 2). Mothers refuse their starving children care (v 3-4), even boiling them for food (v 10). Pure and healthy nobility are filthy, shrivelled and unrecognised (v 7-8). No one is spared, from infants to princes. Status counts for nothing.

- Why do you think the writer highlights these great contrasts?
- What does this teach about trusting in the world's resources?

Greater than Sodom

Read Lamentations 4:6, 9, 11-13

Sodom, a classic example of judgment, was destroyed by God in an instant because of its sinfulness (Genesis 19:24-28). In Israelite thought, it became the epitome of the deserved judgment of God. But Zion's punishment is greater.

- How is it even worse (Lamentations 4:9-10)?
- Notice the people mentioned in verse 13. How does this show us why Jerusalem's sin was worse than Sodom's?
- What is the source of all the destruction (v 11)?

Where priests and prophets lead, the people sooner or later follow. We can be grateful that we have an incorruptible High Priest, who leads us into perfection. But we can also pray for our preachers and pastors today, that they will preach truth rather than politely pastoring people towards destruction.

Read Lamentations 4:14-16

Those priests who could once enter God's temple are now themselves considered unclean (v 14-15). The priests who honoured themselves receive no honour from God; the elders who favoured their own ends receive no favour from God.

Apply

Jerusalem was famous as the place where God dwelled in his temple. It boasted priests and prophets. But it fell.

- How do you, and/or your church, need to hear this warning today?

Bible in a year: Hebrews 1 - 4

Nowhere left to go

Israel often looked to foreign nations for security in good times and rescue in bad.

Look in vain
Read Lamentations 4:17

- *What should they have done (3:25-26)?*

Apply

- *When you are in trouble, where do you tend to turn first?*
- *Lamentations challenged us about this eight days ago! Have you changed in your attitudes since then? How will you change now?*

Relentless enemies
Read Lamentations 4:18-19

The Babylonians watched every step the people made. They cut off every path of escape (v 18). When the city was invaded, the people fled. But the enemy was not content to let them flee (v 19).

- *What freedom did the people have in the city and mountains (v 18-19)?*

TIME OUT

Have you ever felt, or do you ever feel, like this? As though wherever you go and whatever you do, you are still hemmed in by a problem or a temptation or a sin?

Last hope… gone
Read Lamentations 4:20

"The LORD's anointed" was the king. The Lord had promised that King David's family line would reign for ever (see 2 Samuel 7:12-13).

- *What hope did the people put in their king?*
- *What happened to him?*

TIME OUT

Read Luke 1:30-33

- *How did God keep his promise to David of an everlasting kingly line?*

Here is a King who was never, and will never be, "caught in their traps" (Lamentations 4:20)—who we can rely on completely to be our life breath and to give us life breath. We can live safely "under his shadow".

Reversal
Read Lamentations 4:21-22

Here is a message for Jerusalem (Daughter of Zion) and her enemies (Daughter of Edom). Edom is rejoicing while Jerusalem is mourning.

- *How will things be reversed?*
- *What will pass to Edom (v 21)?*

This is a picture of God's judgment (e.g. Isaiah 51:17). All nations and people, sooner or later, must drink this cup. Unless—**read Luke 22:39-44**. Thank Jesus that instead of exposing and judging your wickedness, he took it and was judged for it himself.

Bible in a year: Numbers 25 – 28

A certain restoration

Lamentations ends in prayer for the Lord to look and see what is happening to his people, in hope that he will act soon.

Remember, O Lord

Read Lamentations 5:1

The people are obeying the call in 2:19. They are praying.

- What do they ask the Lord to do?
- What do you think they hope his response will be?
- Why do you think the Lord wants his people to pray? How does prayer honour God?

Paradise lost

Read Lamentations 5:2-6

The good land God prepared for them is now lost. Their men are carried off into exile. Their lives are filled with pain. The exile from Judah is a similar experience to the most catastropic of all exiles, from the perfect Garden of Eden (Genesis 3). Lamentations, of course, sits most neatly on the lips of the Jerusalemites in exile in Babylon. But it is also the song of all who live in exile from the perfect world that humanity was made for—i.e. us.

TIME OUT

Read Revelation 21:1-5

Here is the ultimate end to exile—the recreated Jerusalem, centred on God, with none of the pain and suffering that the writer of Lamentations knew all too well.

Confession of sin

Read Lamentations 5:7-18

- What impact has the previous generation had (v 7)?
- Does this mean that the present generation are innocent (v 16-17)?

We are very good at finding excuses for our sin. But, whatever others have done, our sin is still our sin. And it needs to be confessed so that we can cry for mercy.

Pray

Look honestly at your life, and confess your sins to God now. Then **read 1 John 1:9**.

You reign!

Read Lamentations 5:19-22

God's reign depends on nothing outside of himself. No one can compel him to act. All that sinful humans can do is ask for restoration.

- What exactly do the people ask for (v 21)?
- What do they fear has happened (v 22)?

They do not know how the story ends. We do. The exile was partially ended with the return of the people to the land, began to be fully ended with the resurrection of Jesus and the start of the church, and will be fully over when we enjoy life in the new Jerusalem. We enjoy certainty which the writer of verse 23 could not. We know we will never be rejected.

Bible in a year: 2 Chronicles 6 – 10

Plain and Simple Bible Devotions

Using short sentences and simple language, these 30-day devotionals are ideal for those who would appreciate concise devotions that are easy to understand. They will help users to get into the Bible and grow in faith. They can be used individually or with others.

- Short sentences that are easy to read
- Simple language that is easy to understand
- Each devotion is just two pages long with large typeface and wide spacing
- Useful for anyone who may find reading longer devotions difficult

thegoodbook.co.uk/explore-the-life-of-jesus
thegoodbook.com/explore-the-life-of-jesus
thegoodbook.com.au/explore-the-life-of-jesus

Introduce a friend to
explore

If you're enjoying using *Explore*, why not introduce a friend? Time with God is our introduction to daily Bible reading and is a great way to get started with a regular time with God. It includes 28 daily readings along with articles, advice and practical tips on how to apply what the passage teaches.

Why not order a copy for someone you would like to encourage?

Coming up next...

- Judges
  with Timothy Keller

- 2 Kings
  with Paul Mathole

- 2 Corinthians
  with Gary Millar

- Christmas
  with Christopher Ash

- Psalms
  with Carl Laferton and Tim Thornborough

Don't miss your copy. Contact your local Christian bookshop or church agent, or visit:

UK & Europe: thegoodbook.co.uk
info@thegoodbook.co.uk
Tel: +44 (0) 333 123 0880

North America: thegoodbook.com
info@thegoodbook.com
Tel: +1 866 244 2165

Australia & New Zealand:
thegoodbook.com.au
info@thegoodbook.com.au
Tel: +61 (0) 9564 3555

South Africa: www.christianbooks.co.za
orders@christianbooks.co.za
Tel: +27 (0) 21 674 6931/2